SKULL
COLORING BOOK
FOR ADULTS

▲ ART THERAPY COLORING

Preview of Coloring Pages

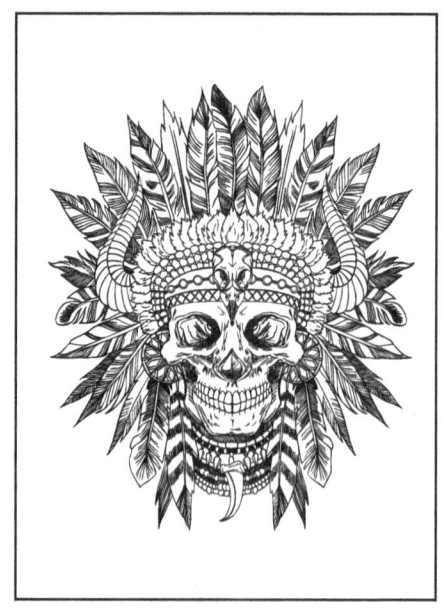
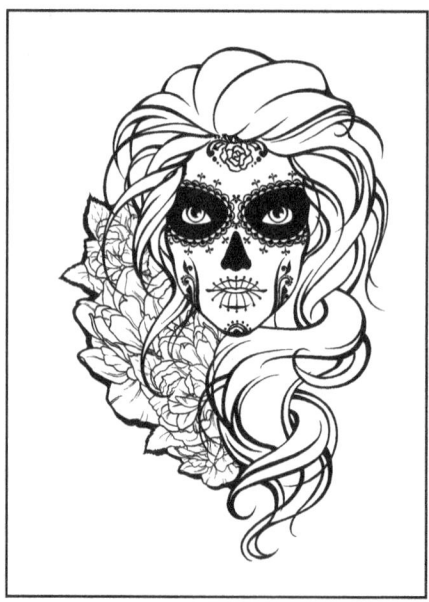
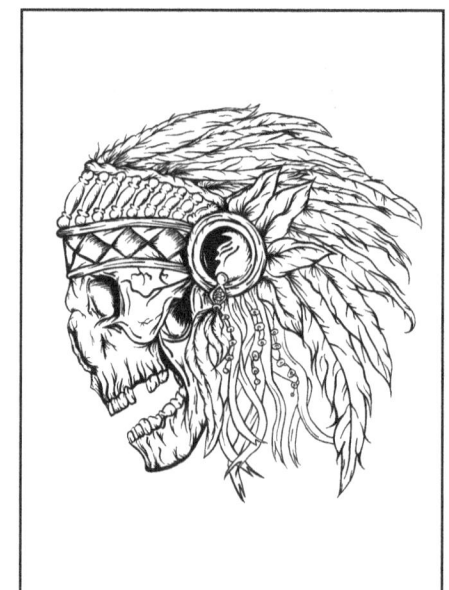
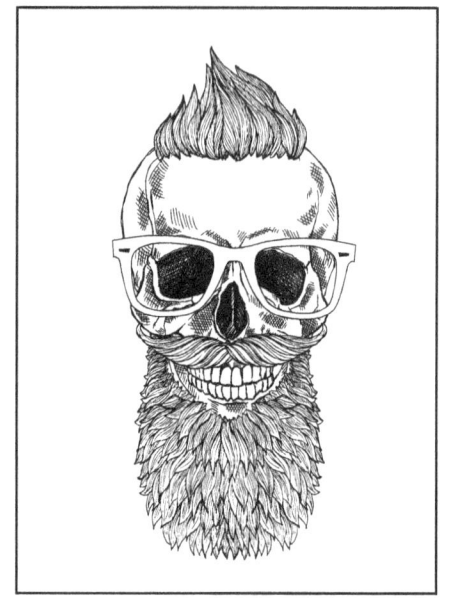
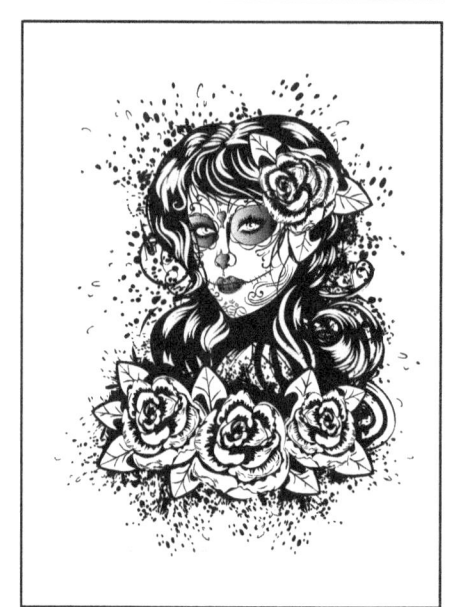
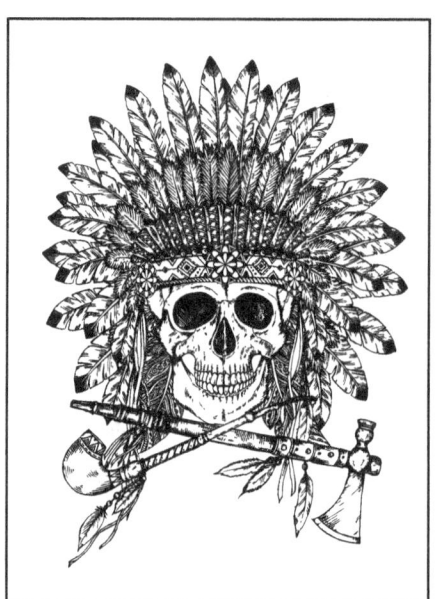
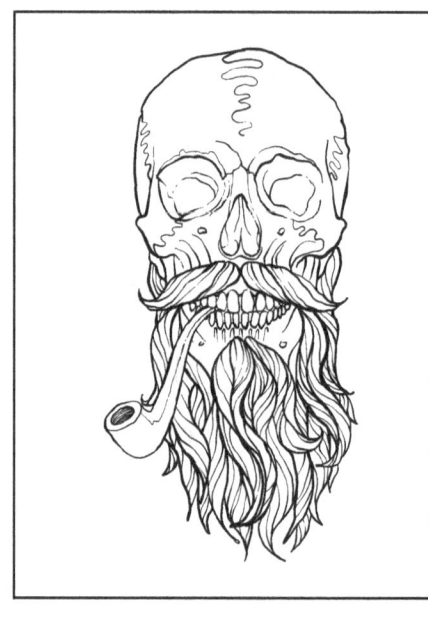
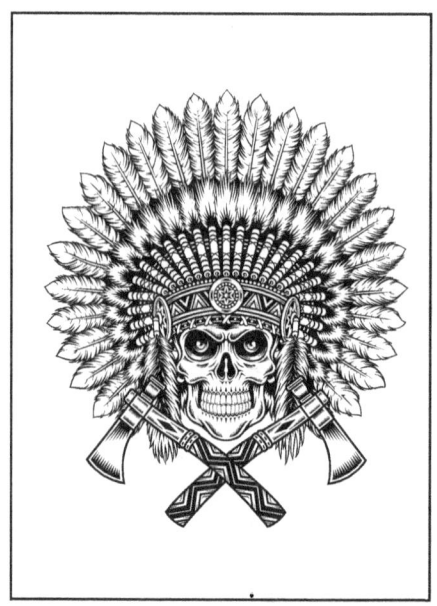
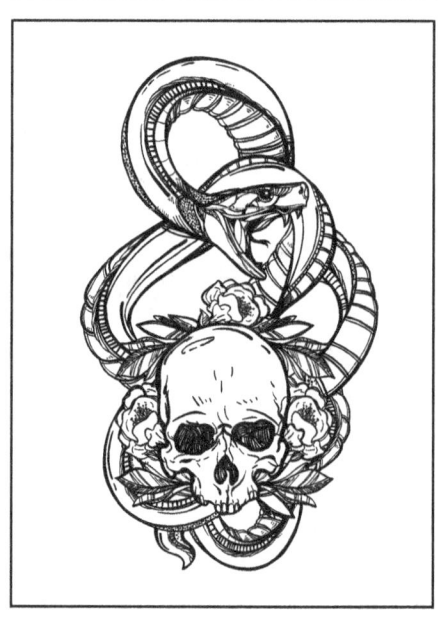

www.arttherapycoloring.com

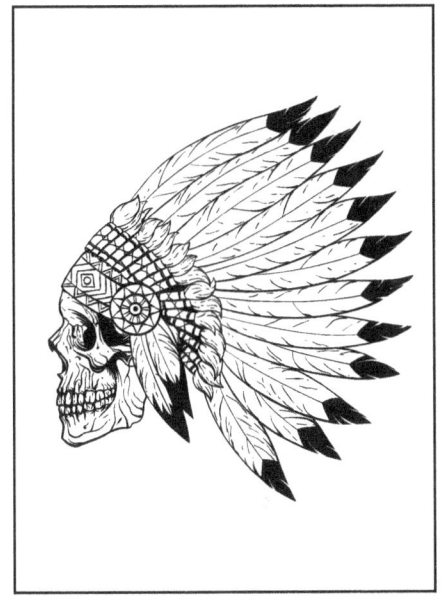
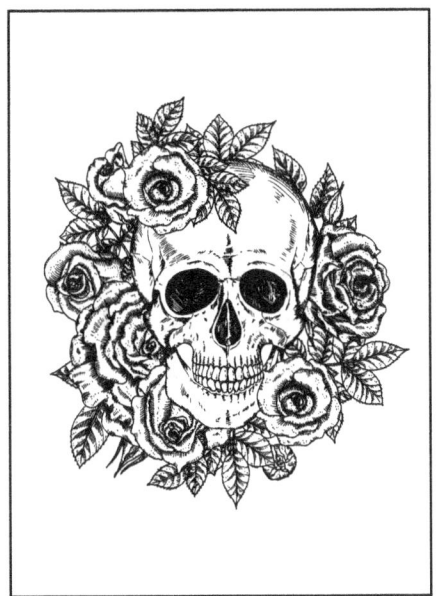
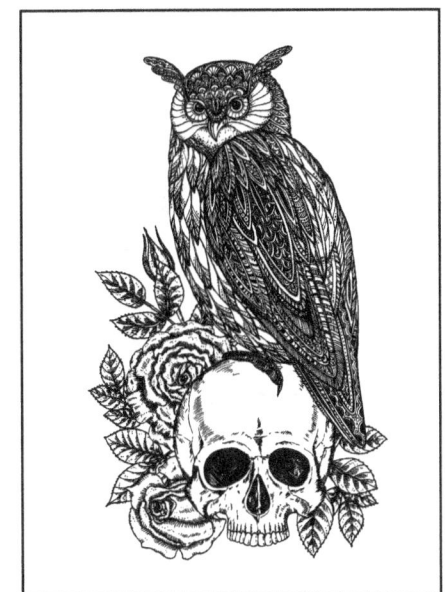
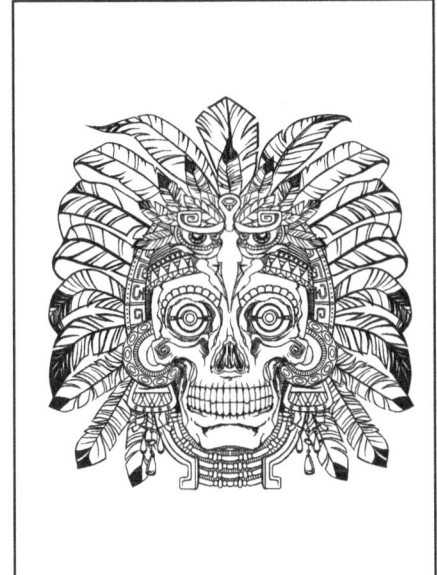
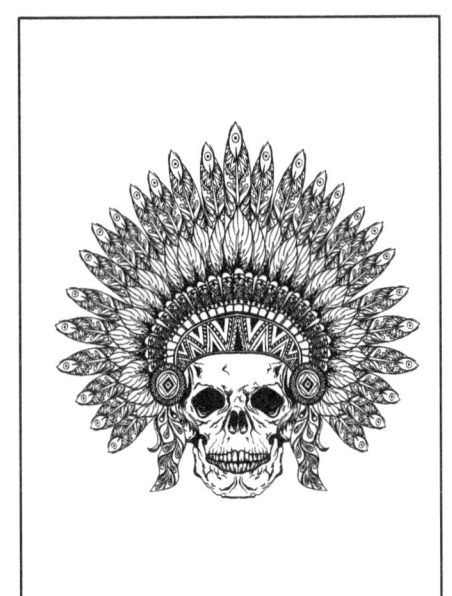
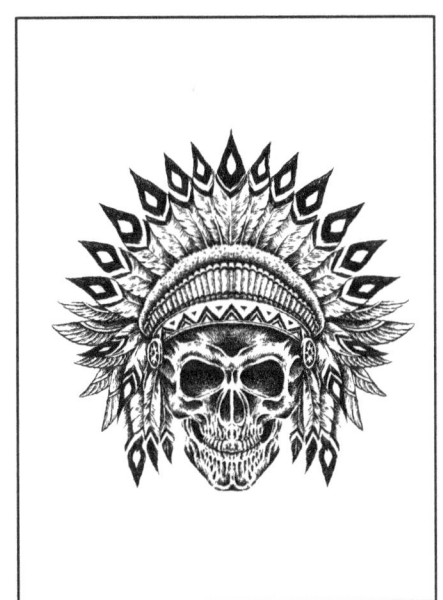
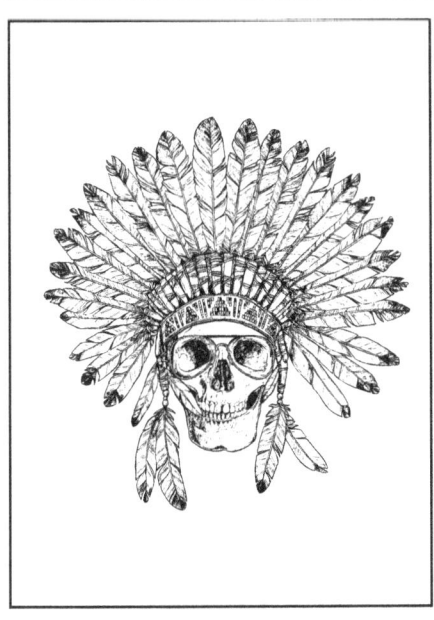
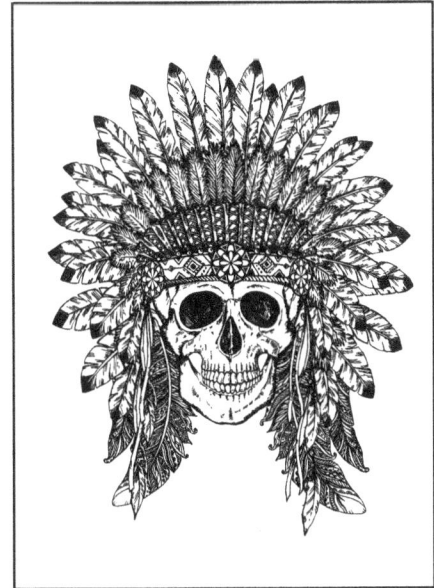
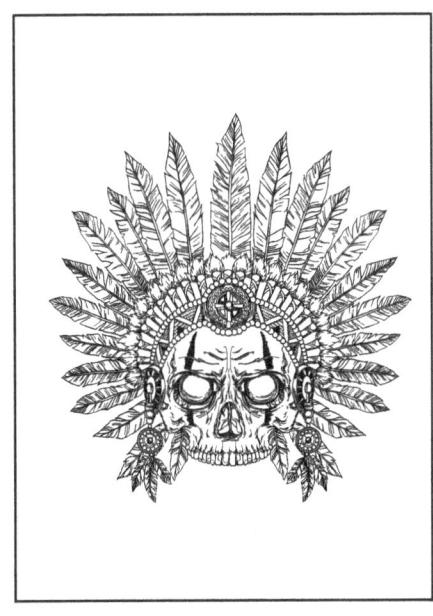

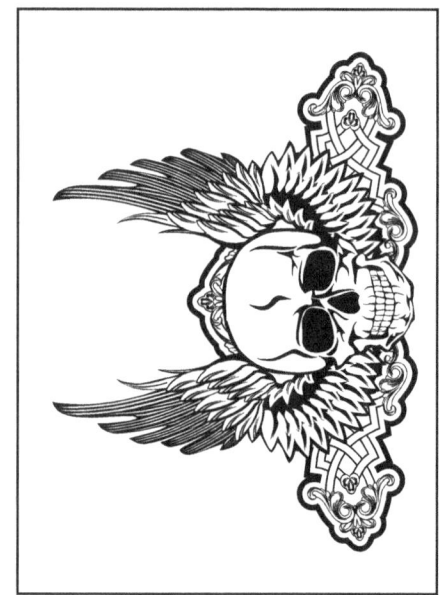
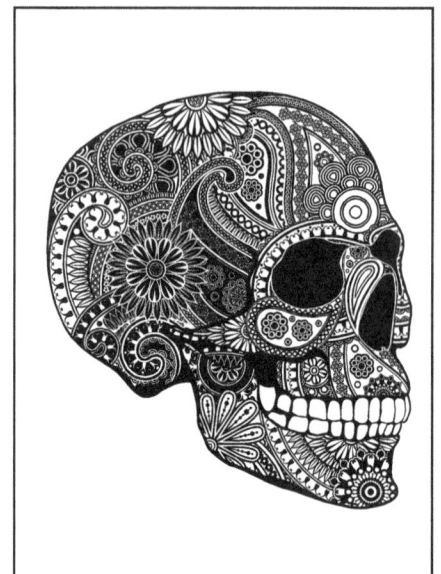
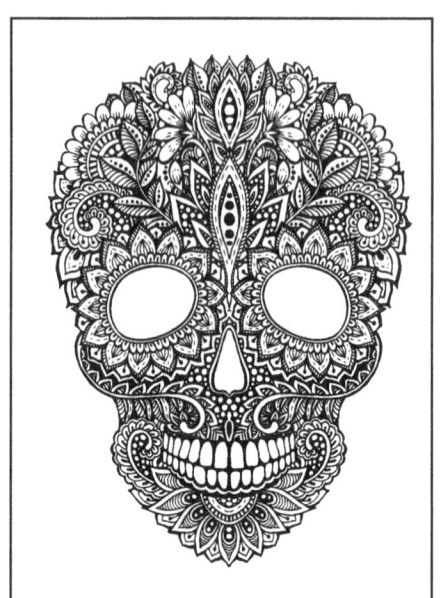
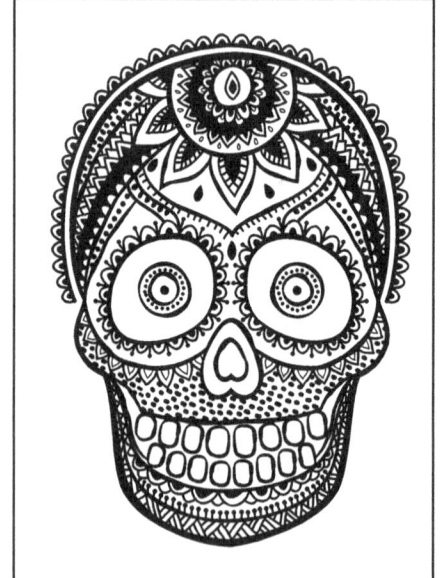
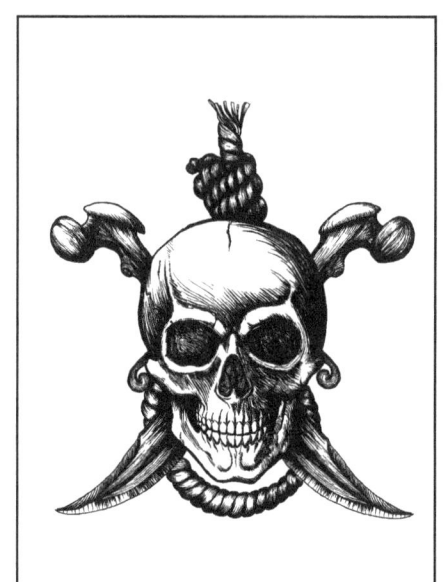
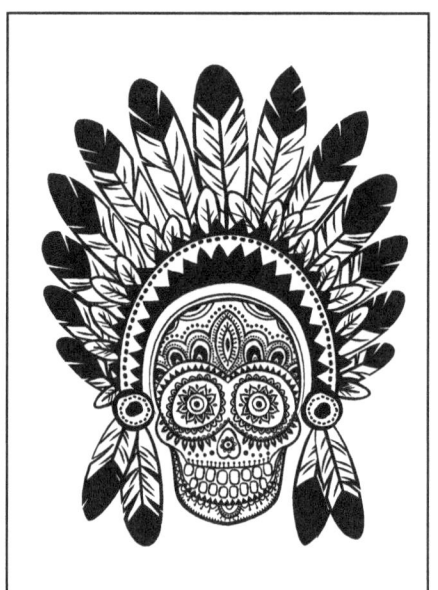
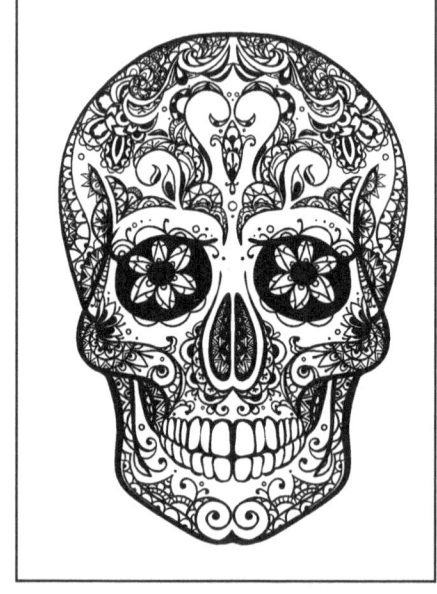
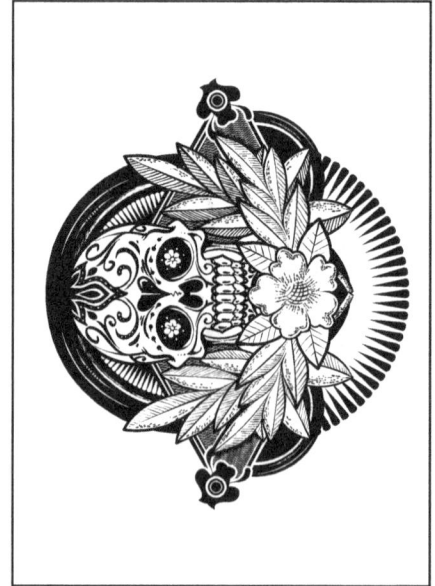
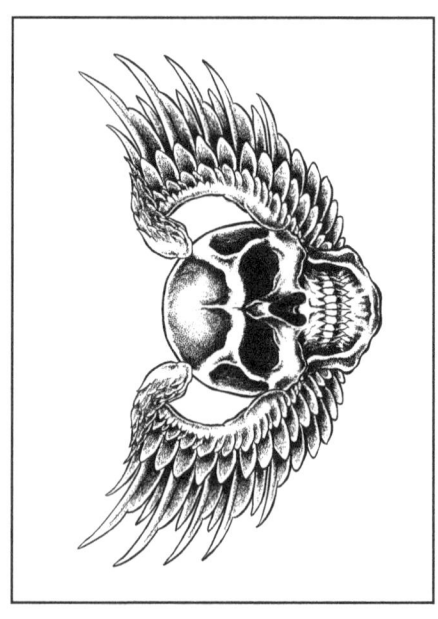

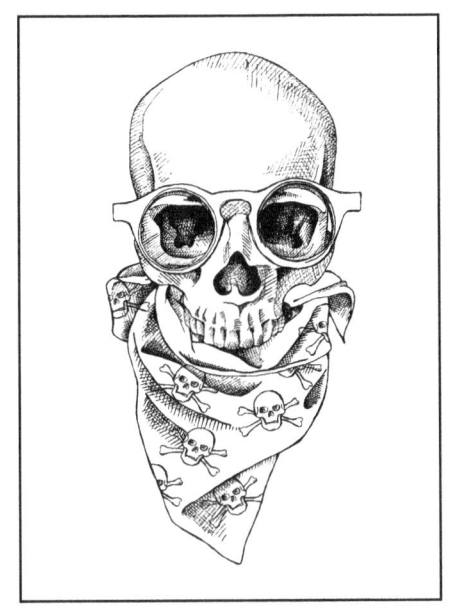
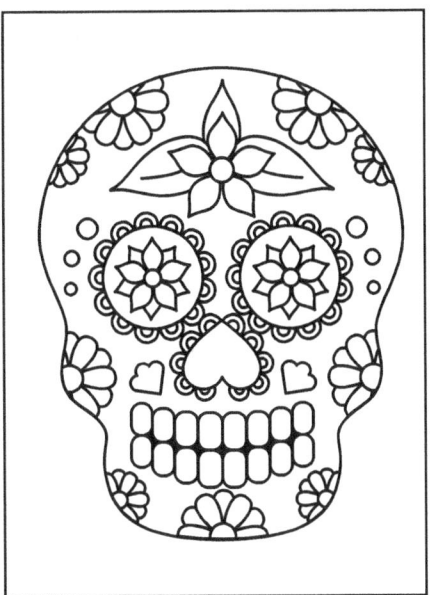
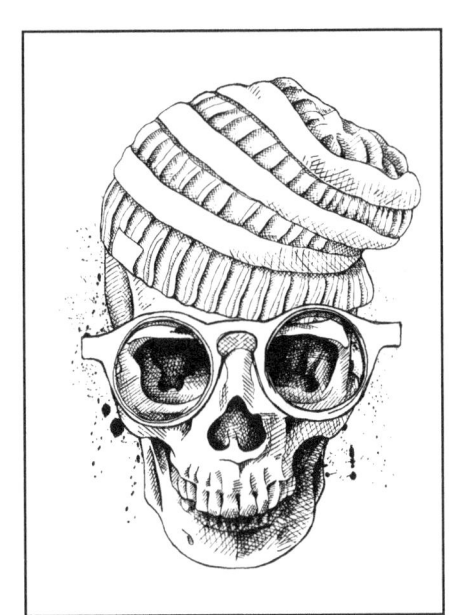
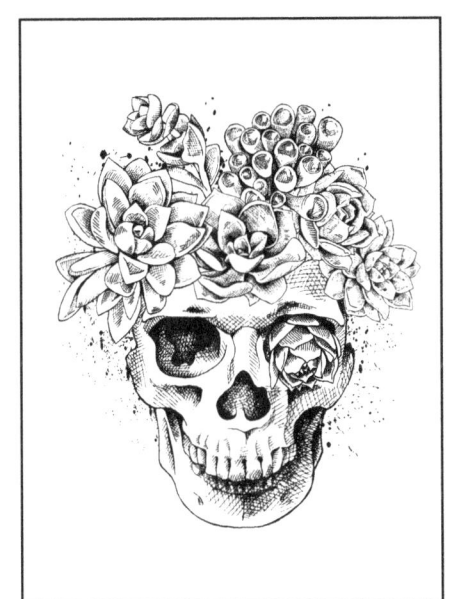
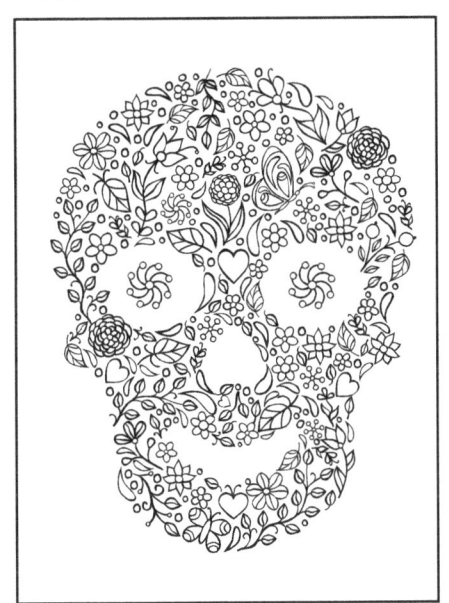
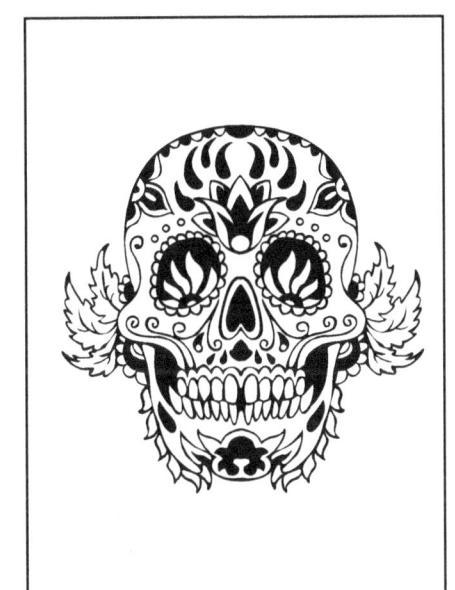
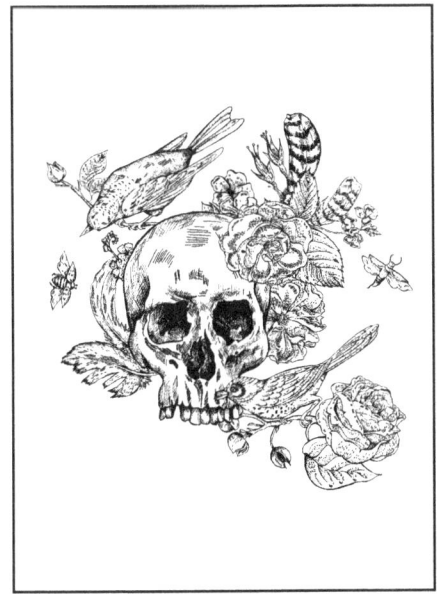
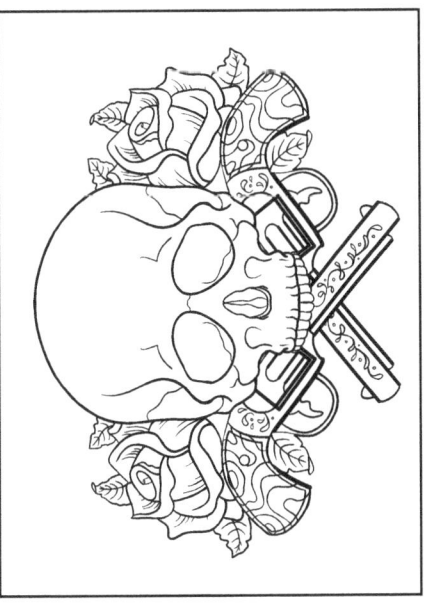
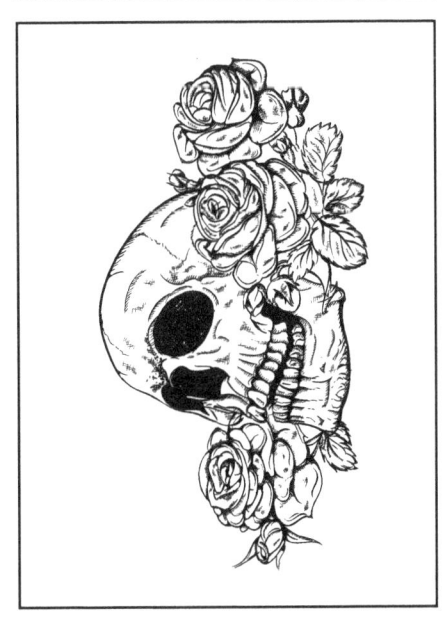

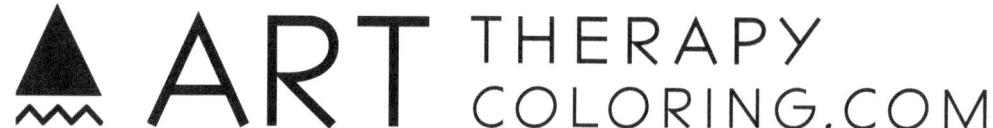

Did You Enjoy Our Coloring Book?

We Want To Hear About It!

Help spread the word about our adult coloring books! We give 10% of all proceeds from Art Therapy products to benefit pancreatic cancer patients and their families.

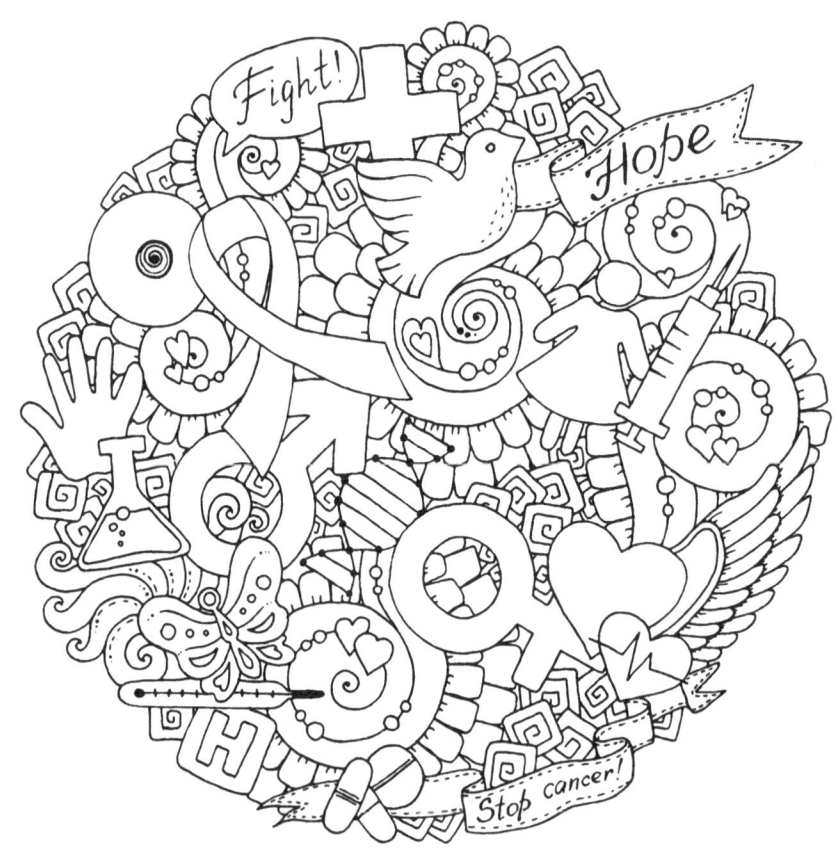

The best way to spread the word is through reviews. We know how busy you are, especially with all of that coloring, but we would appreciate it!

Visit our website at **www.arttherapycoloring.com**

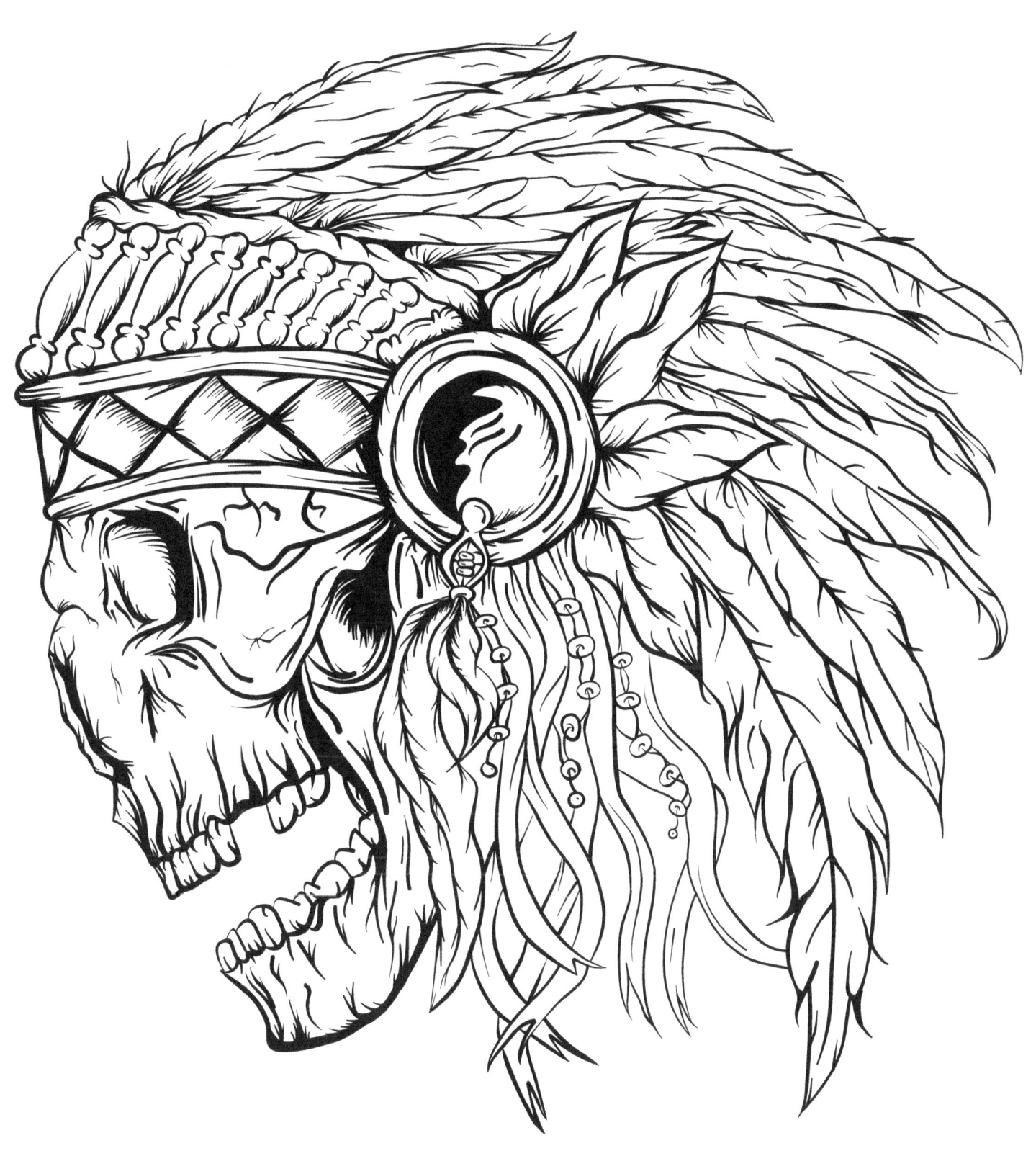

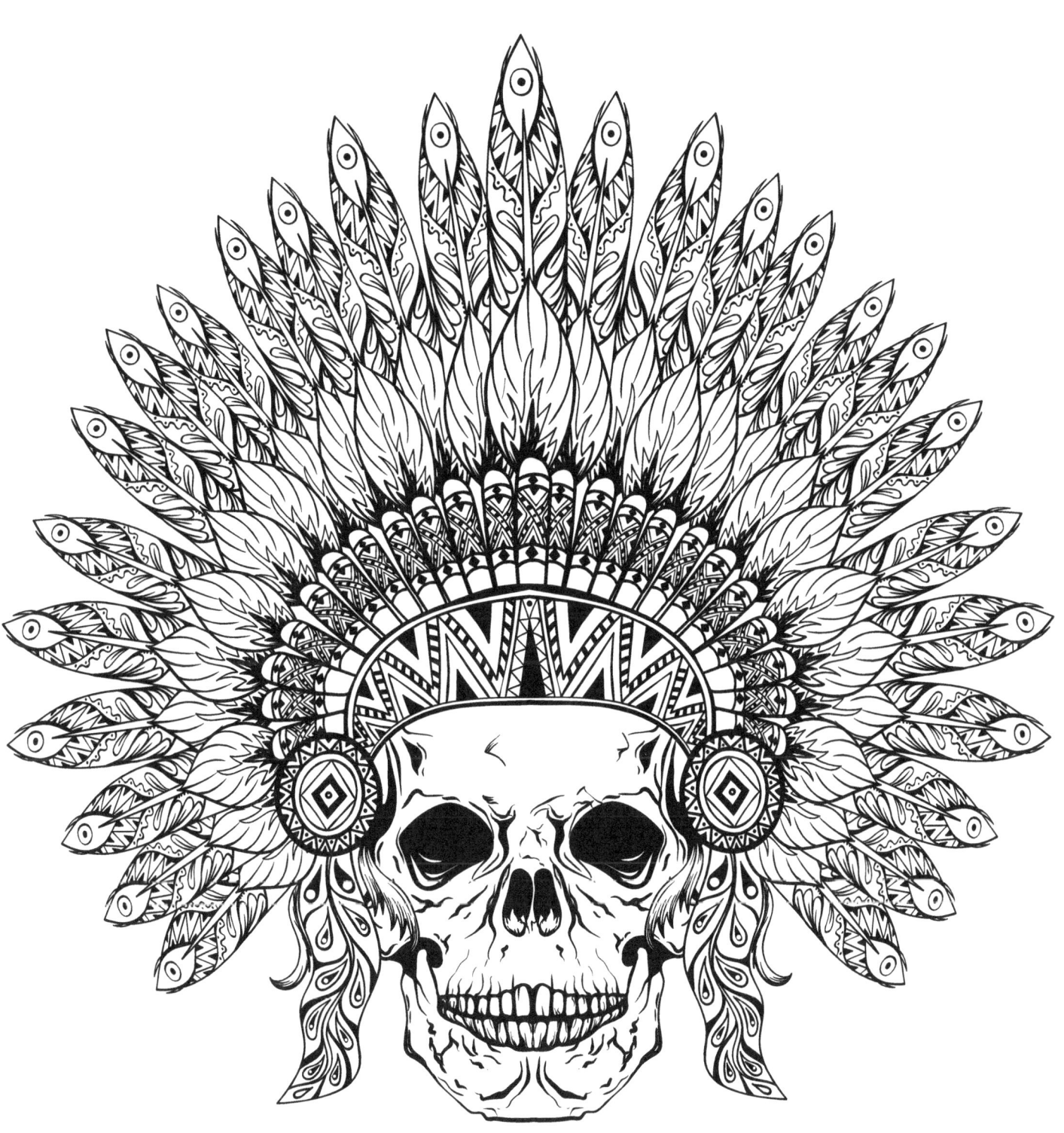

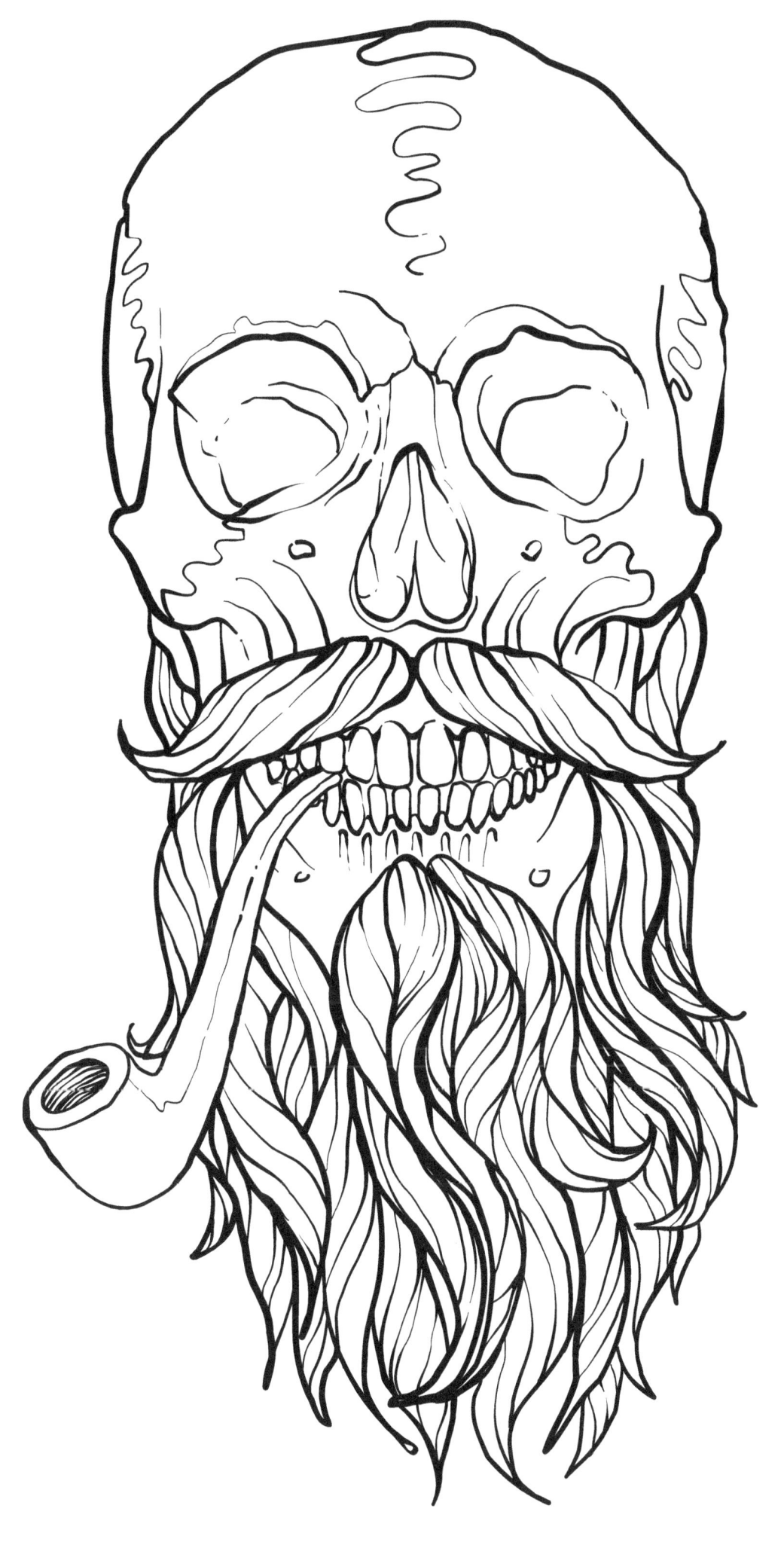

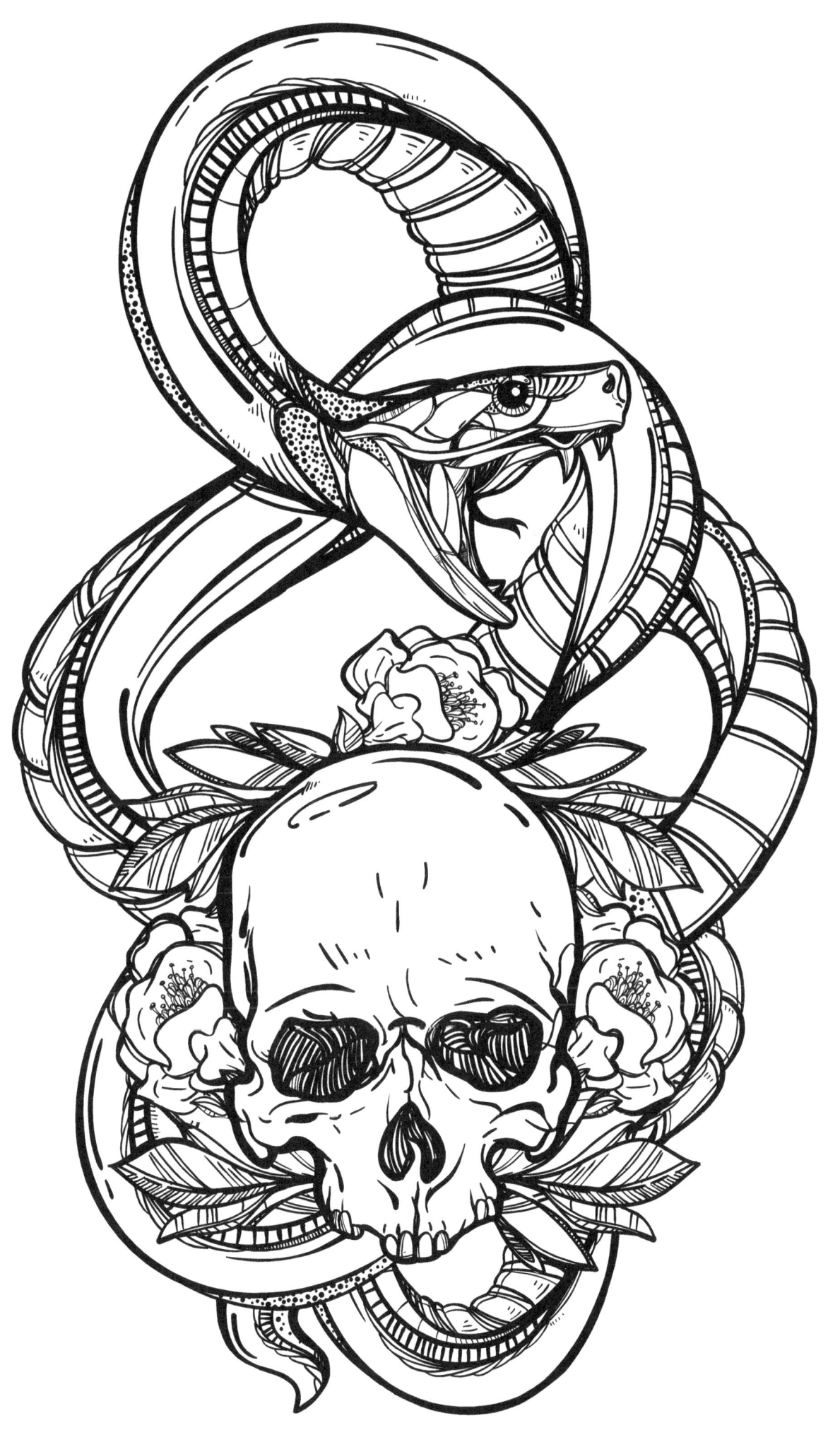

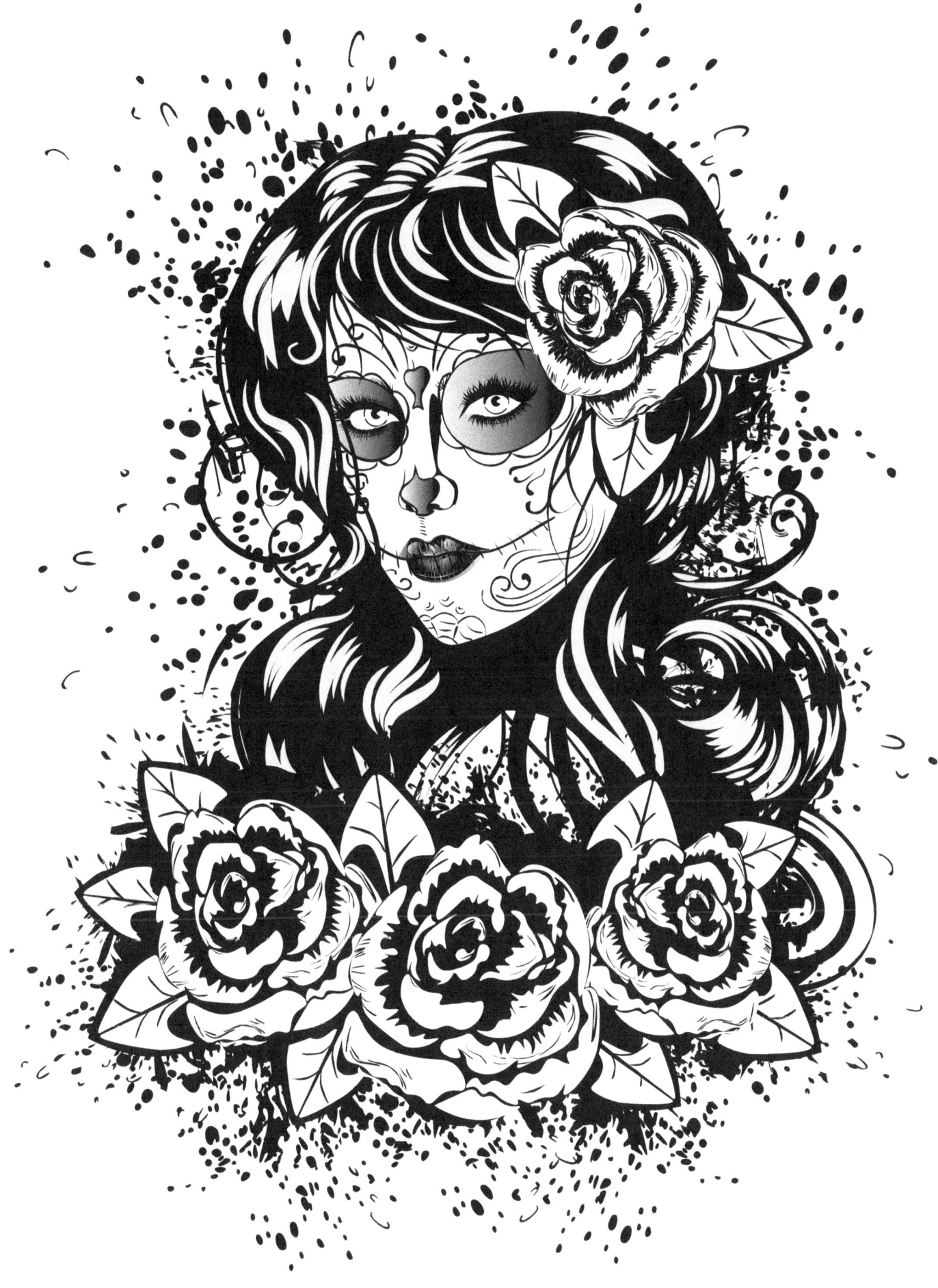

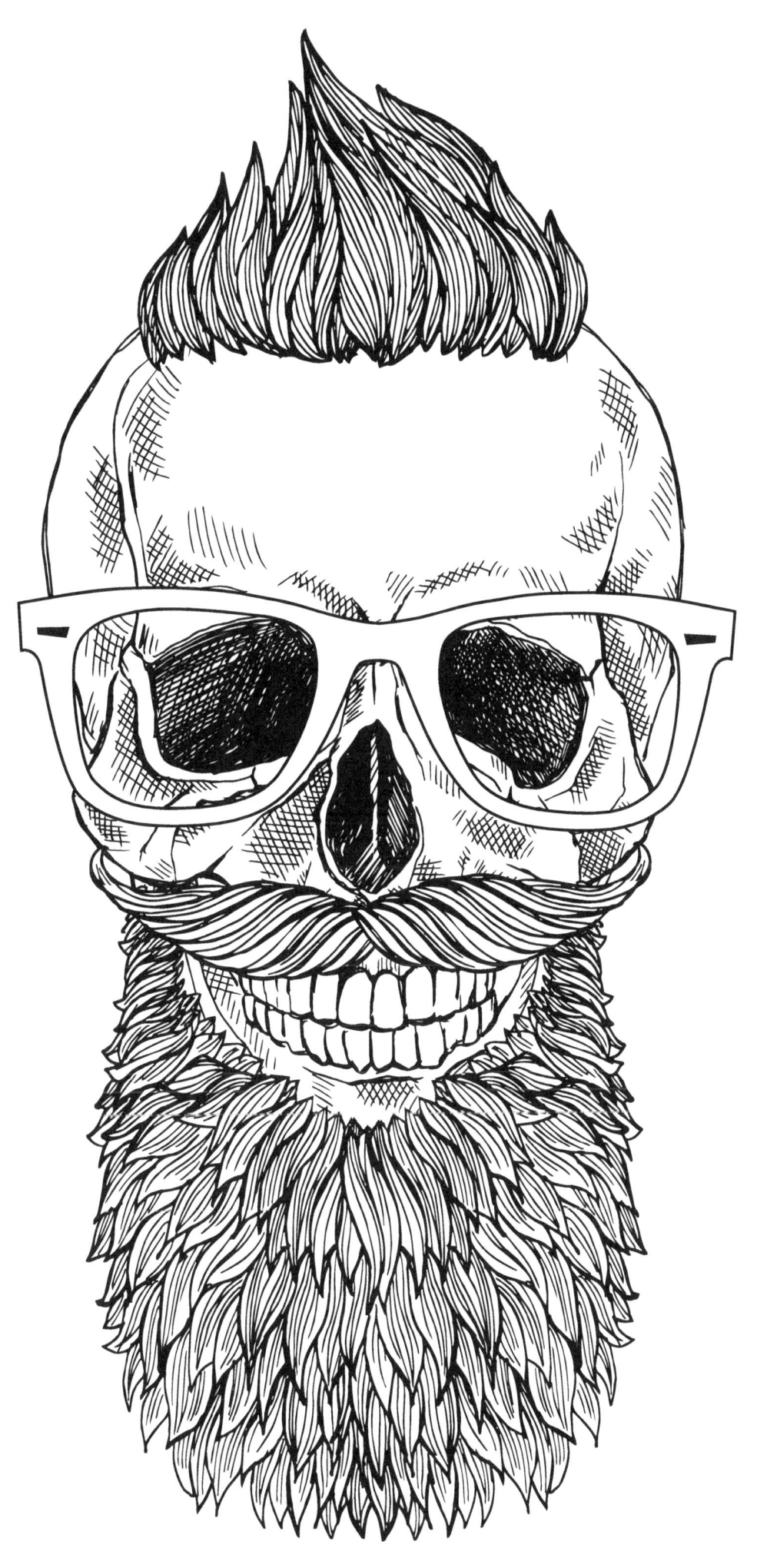

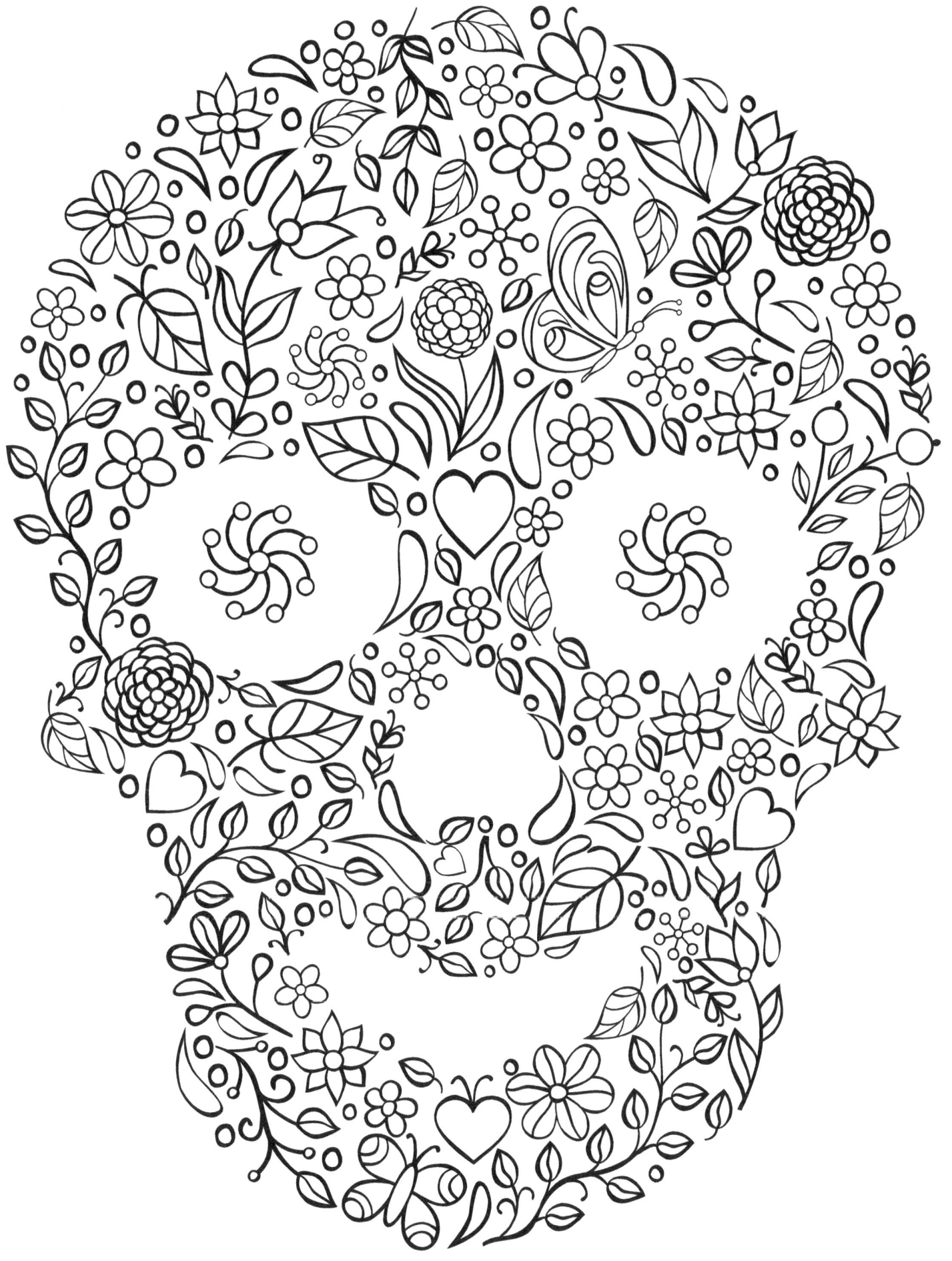

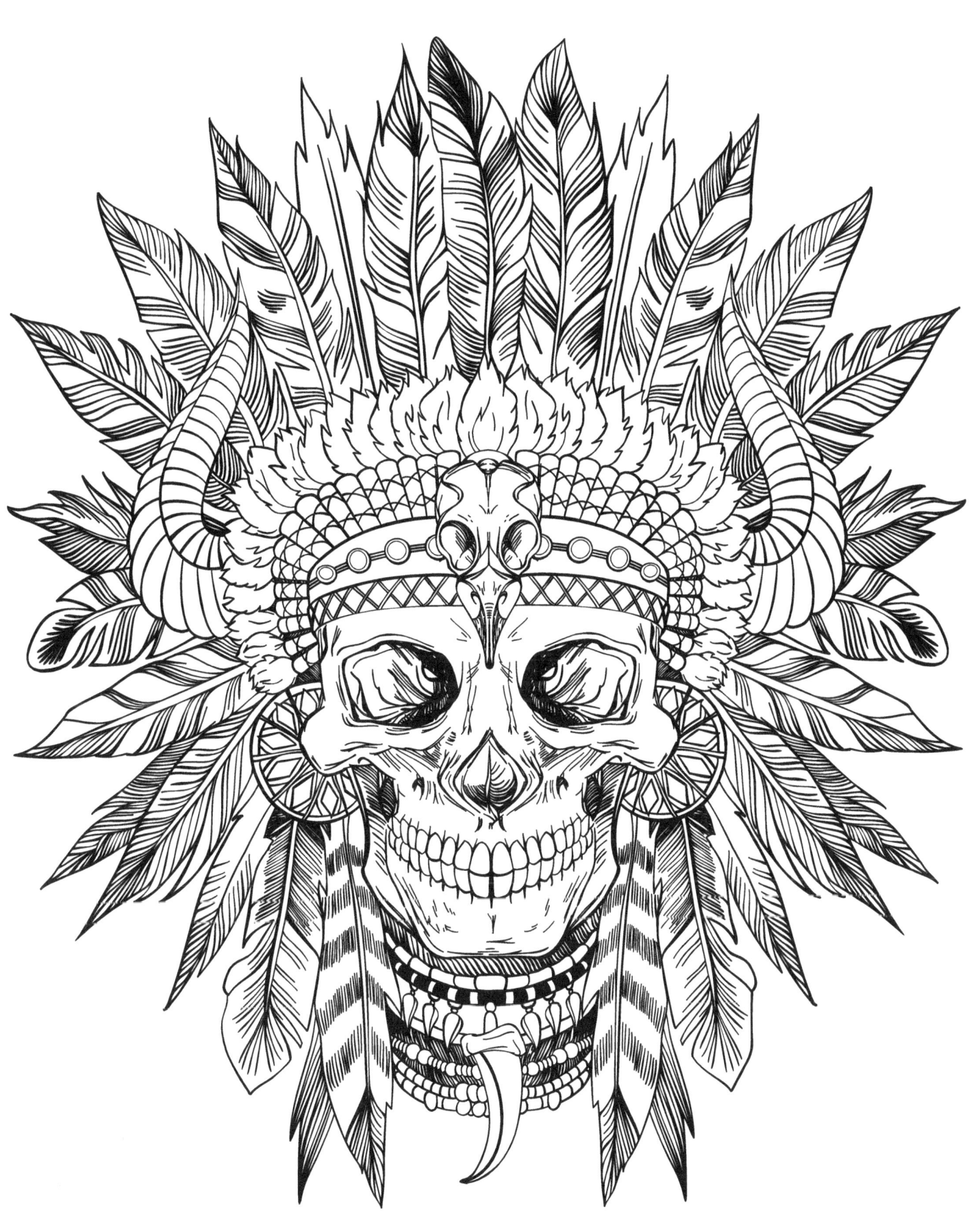

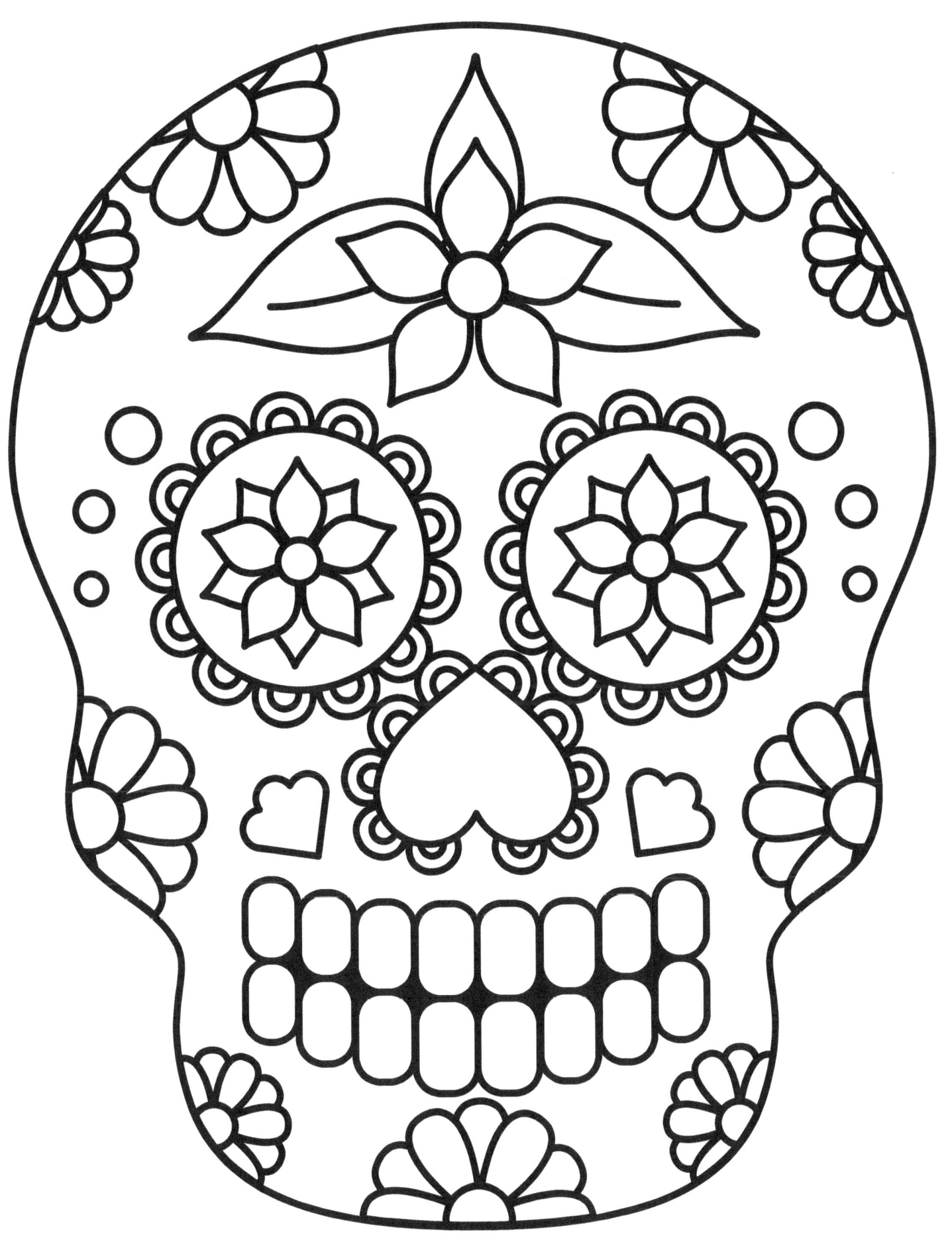

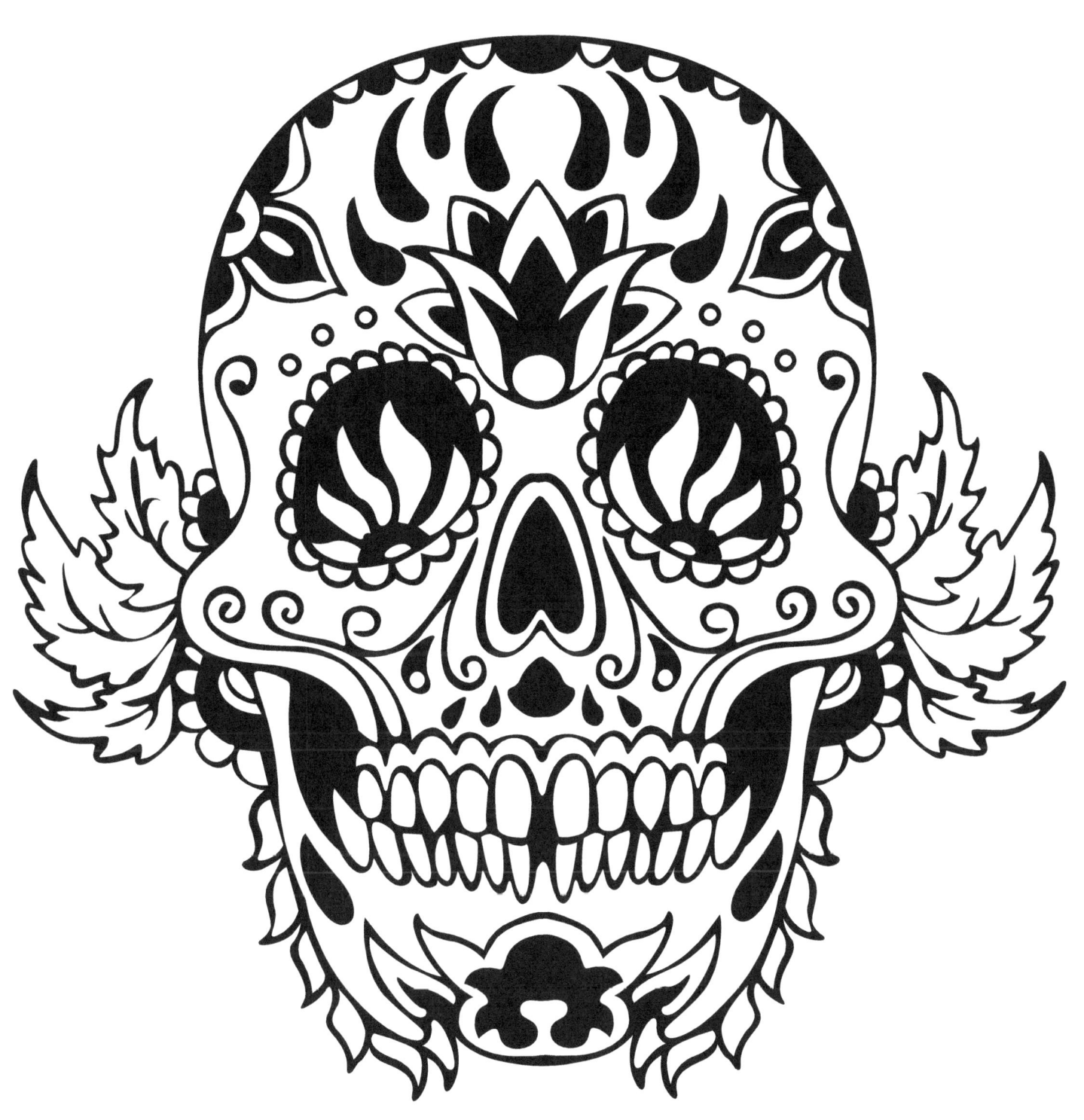

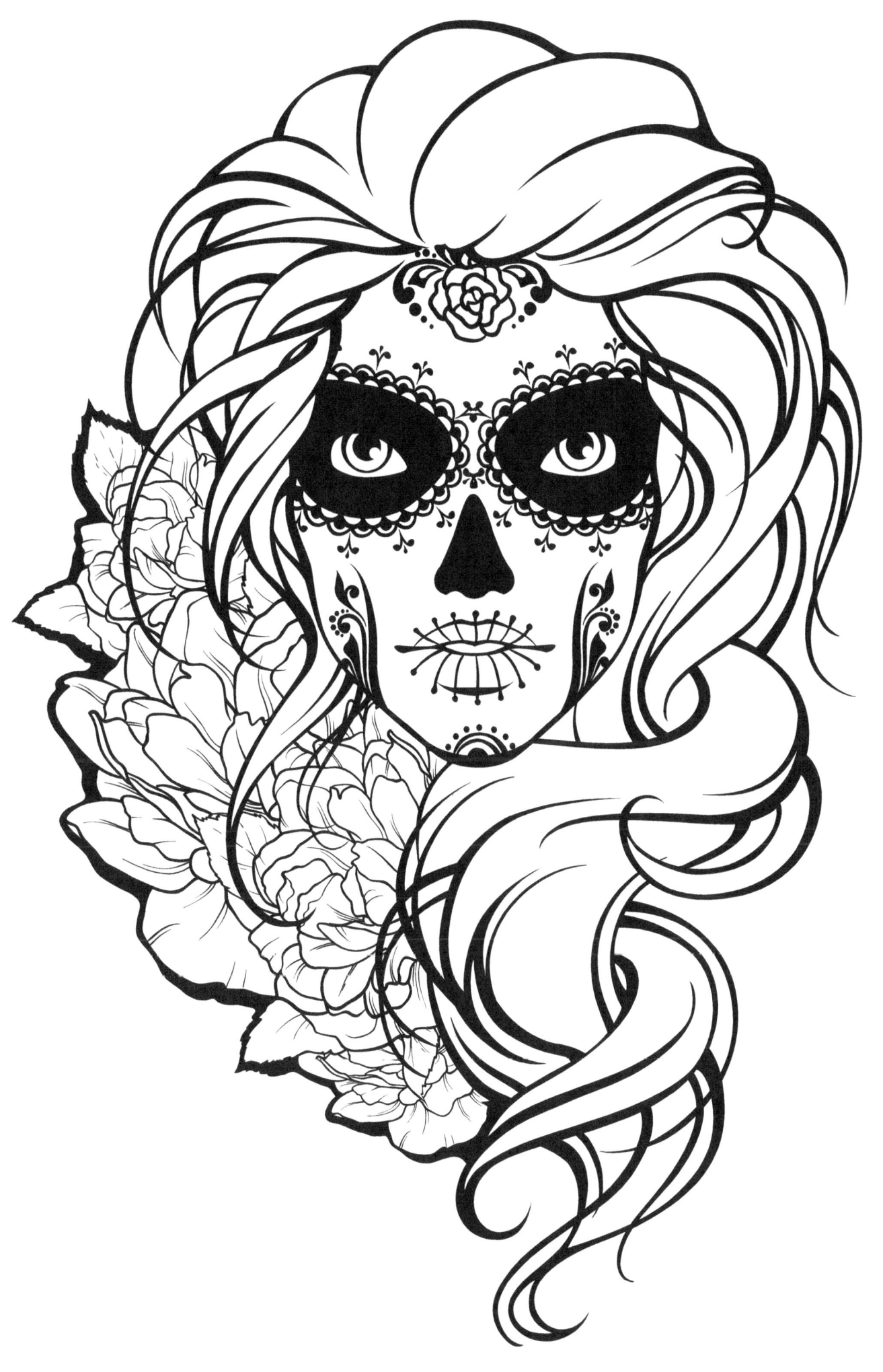

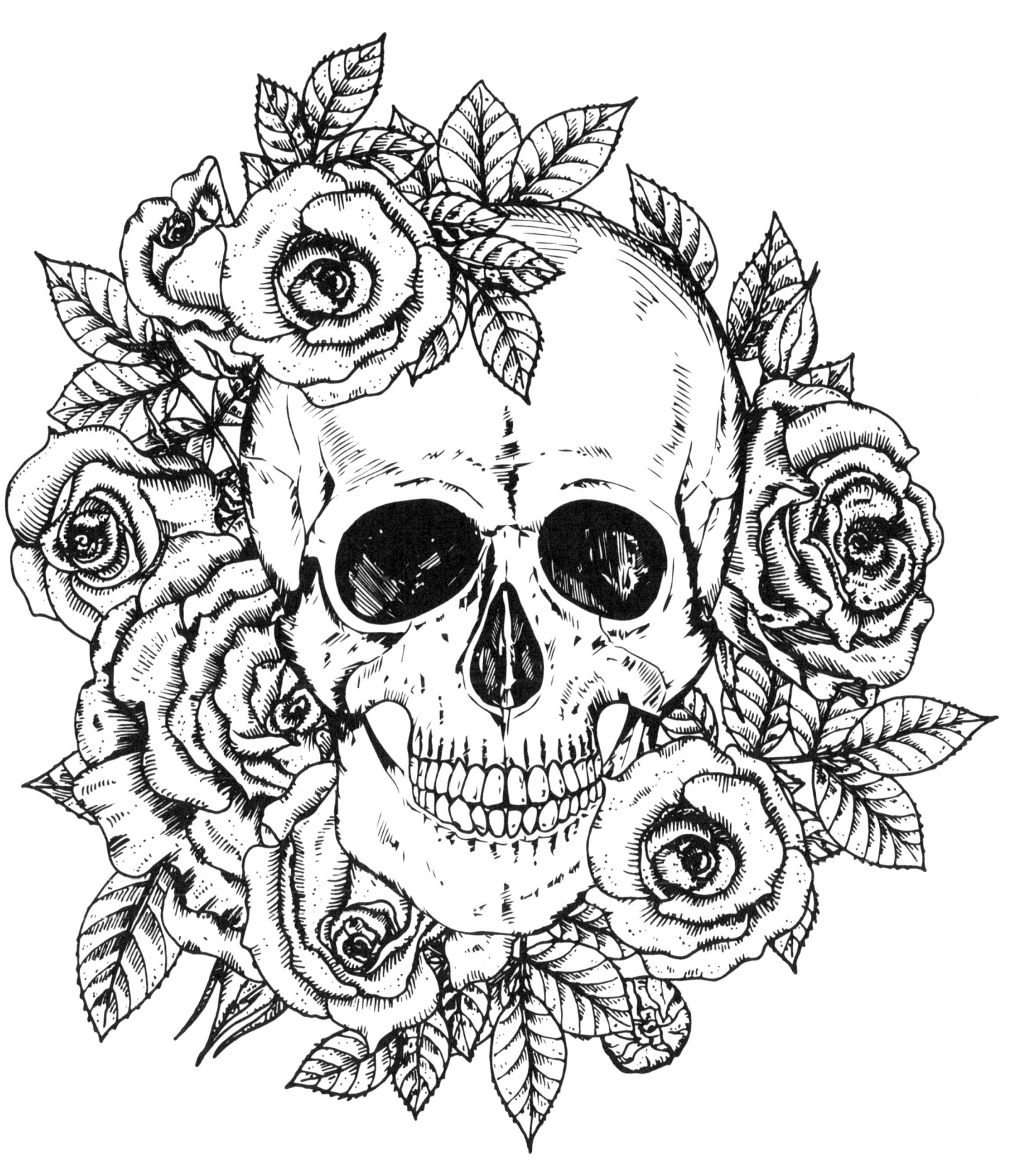

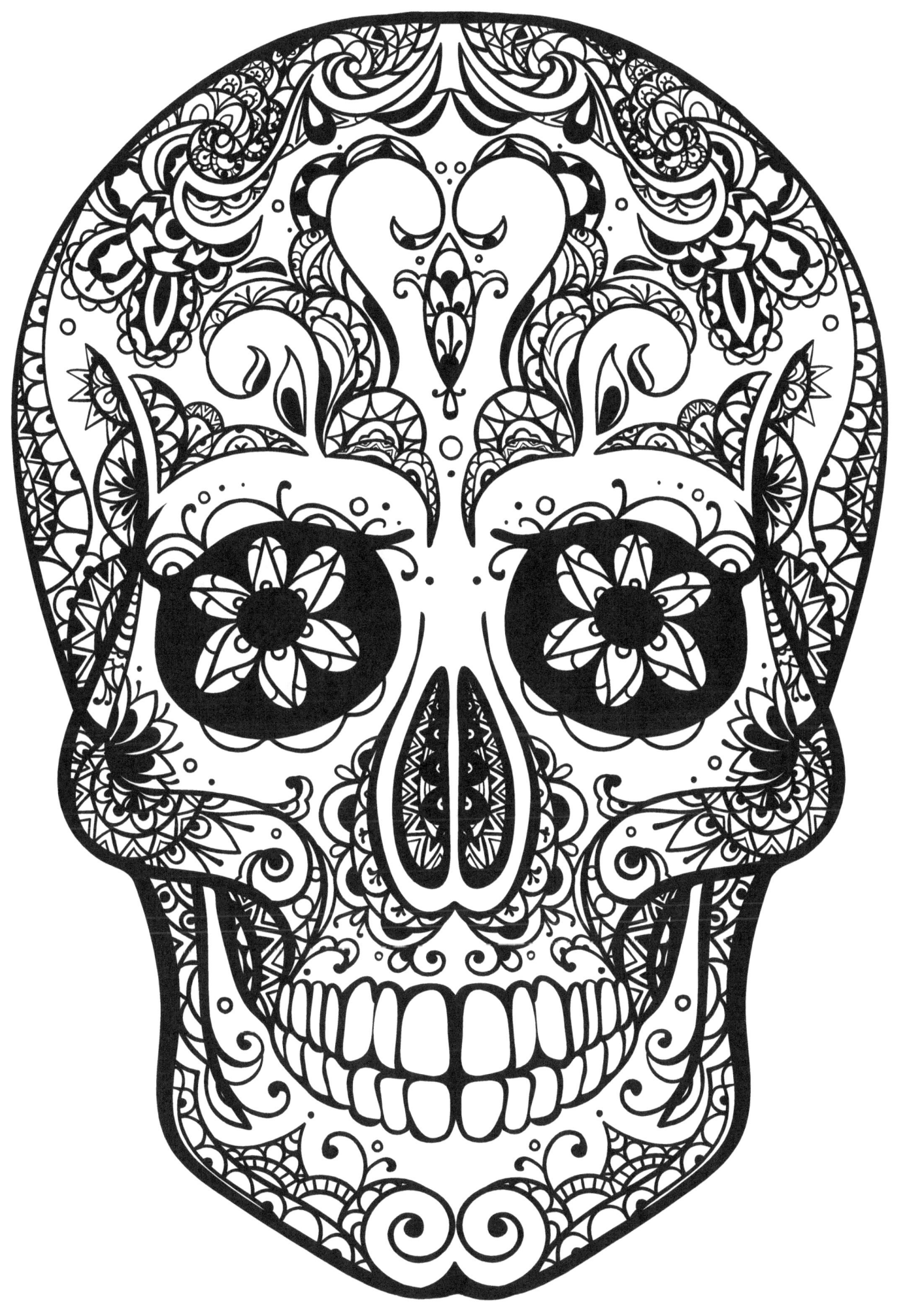

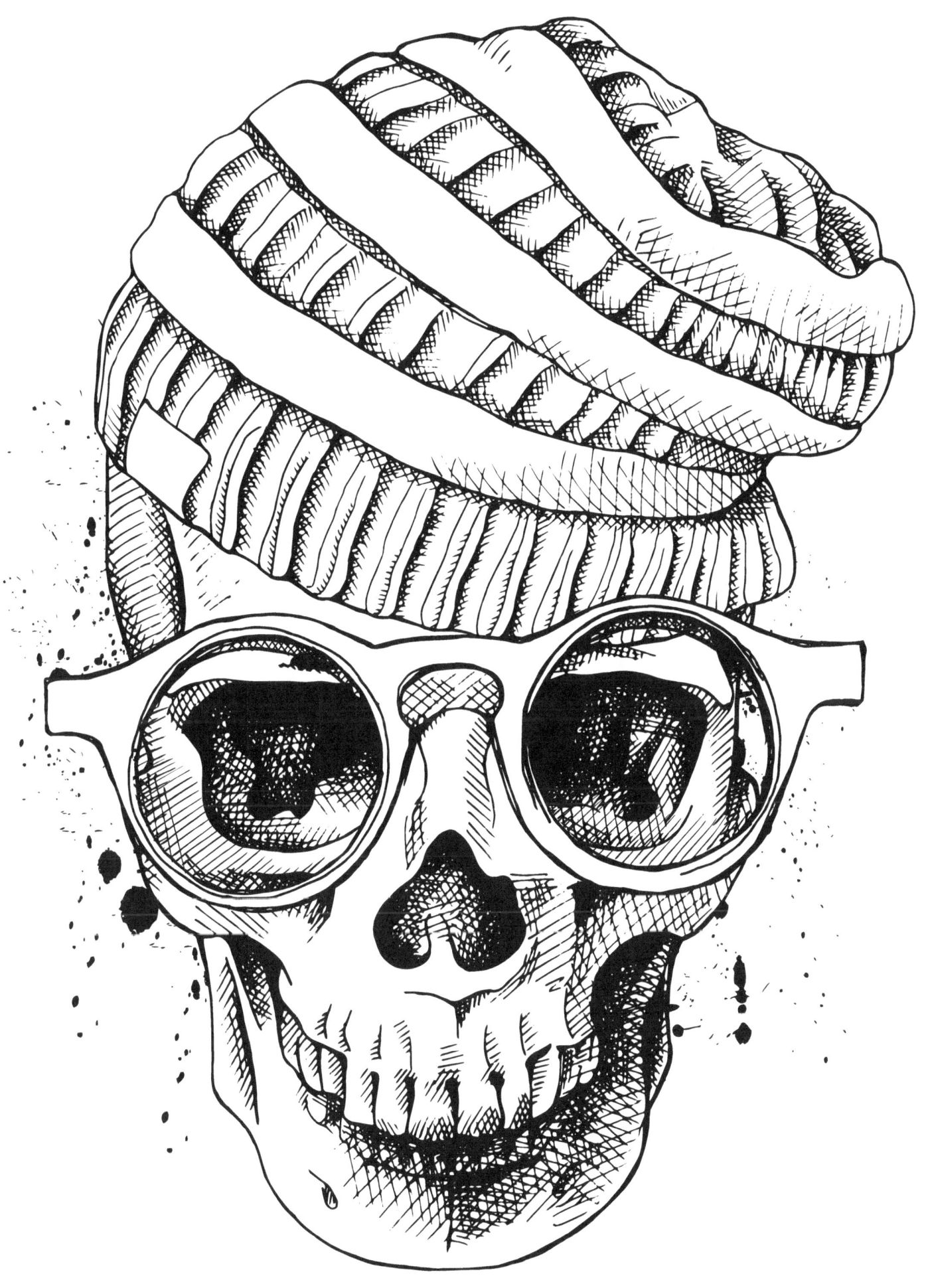

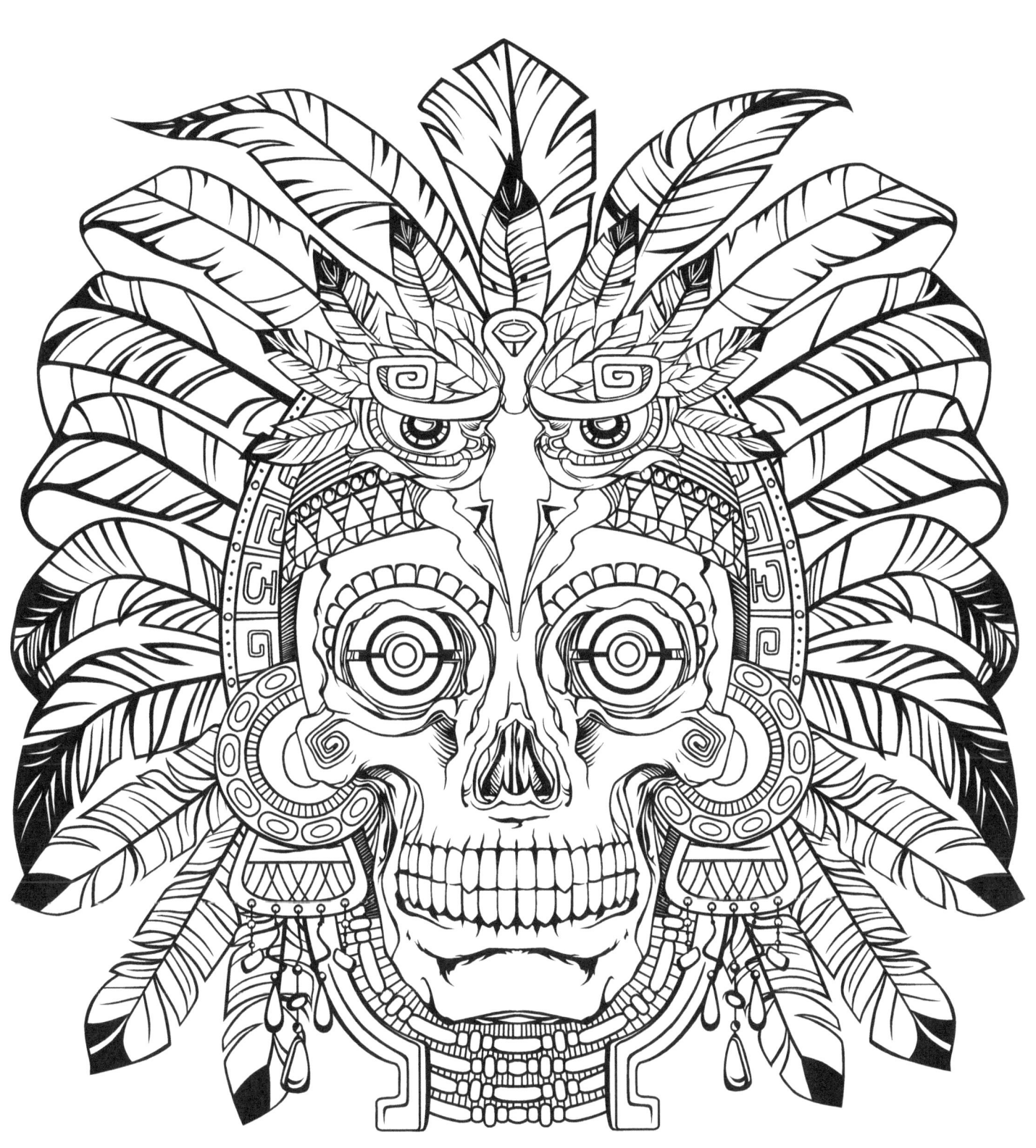

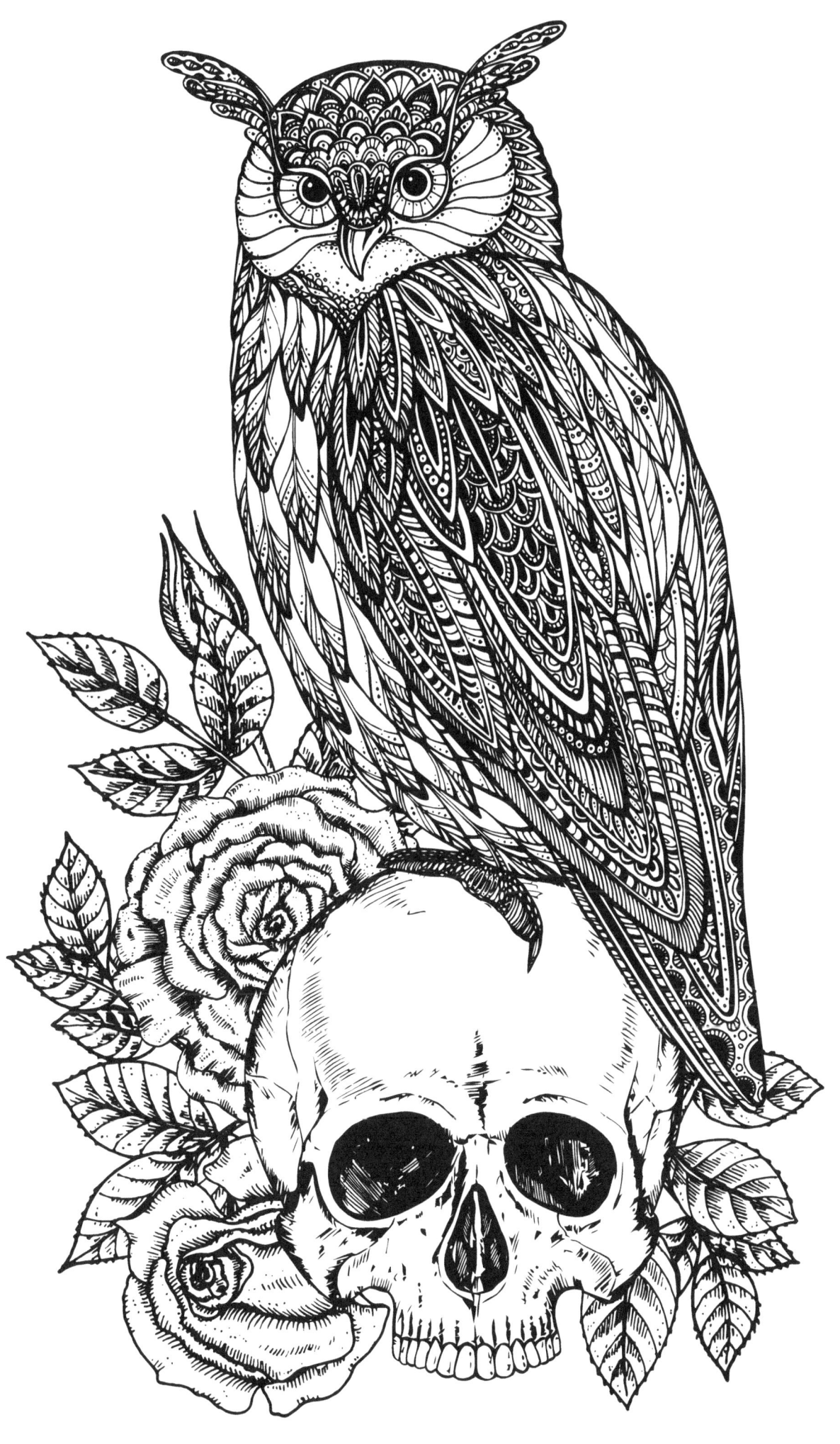

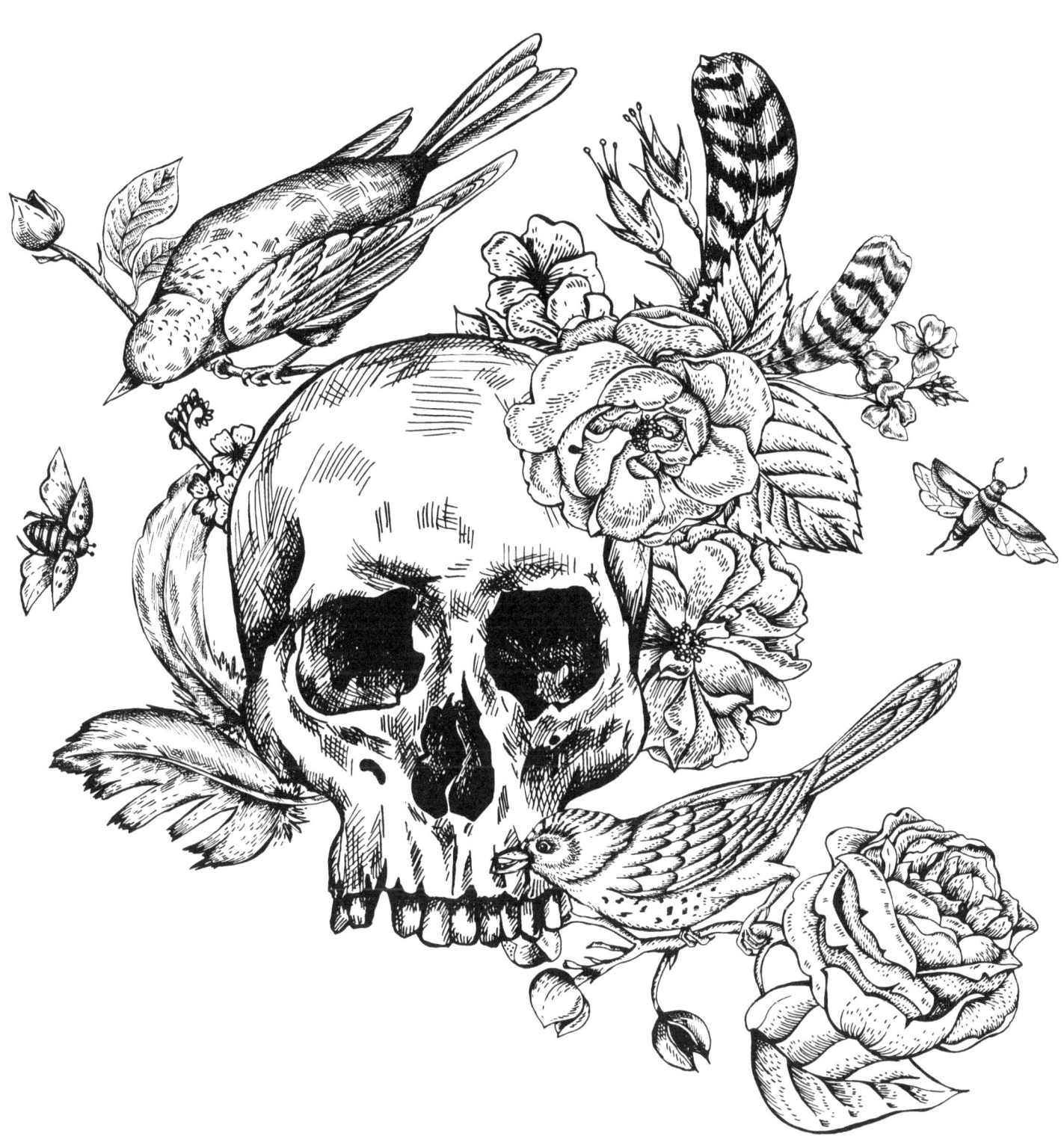

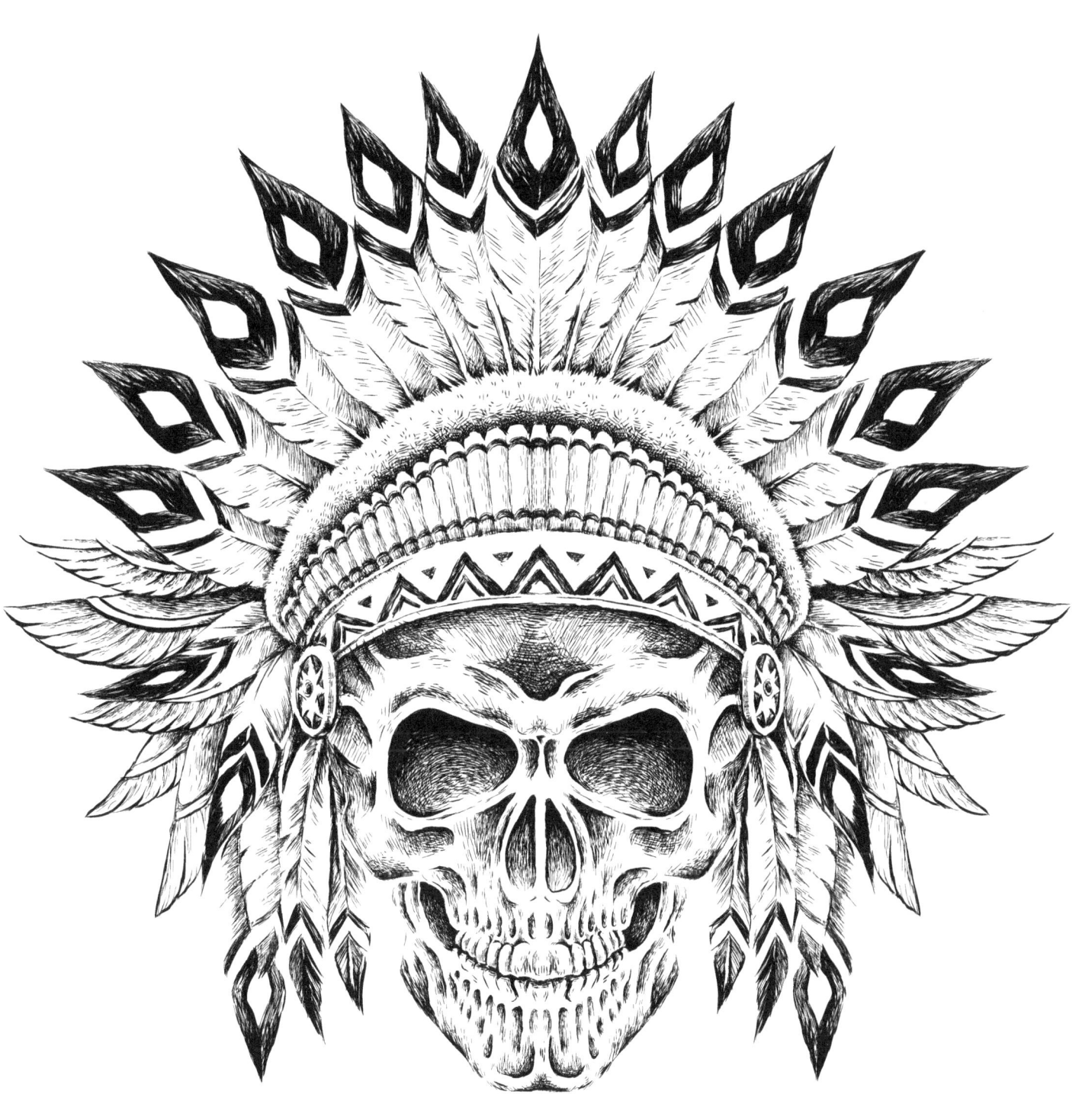

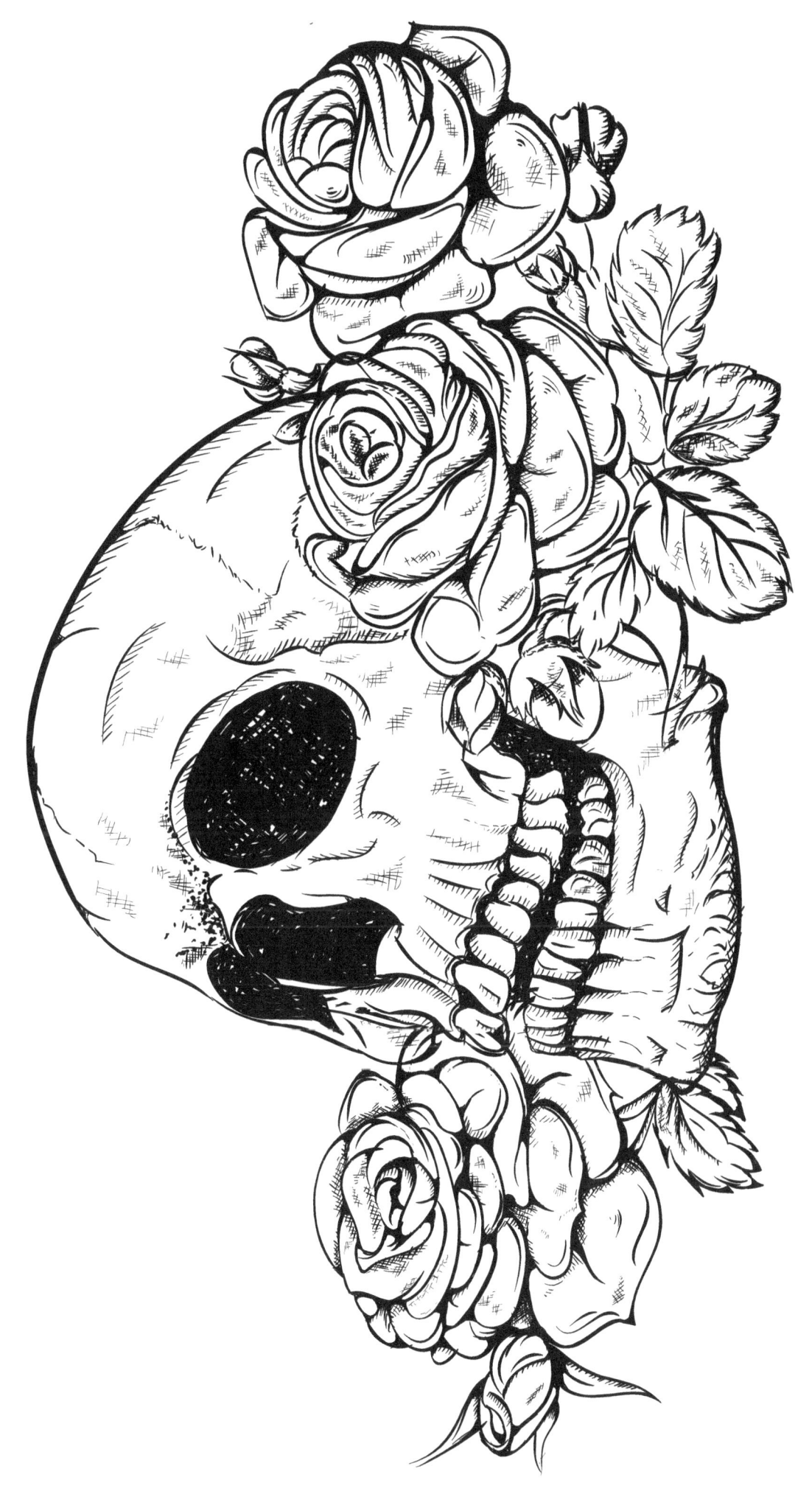

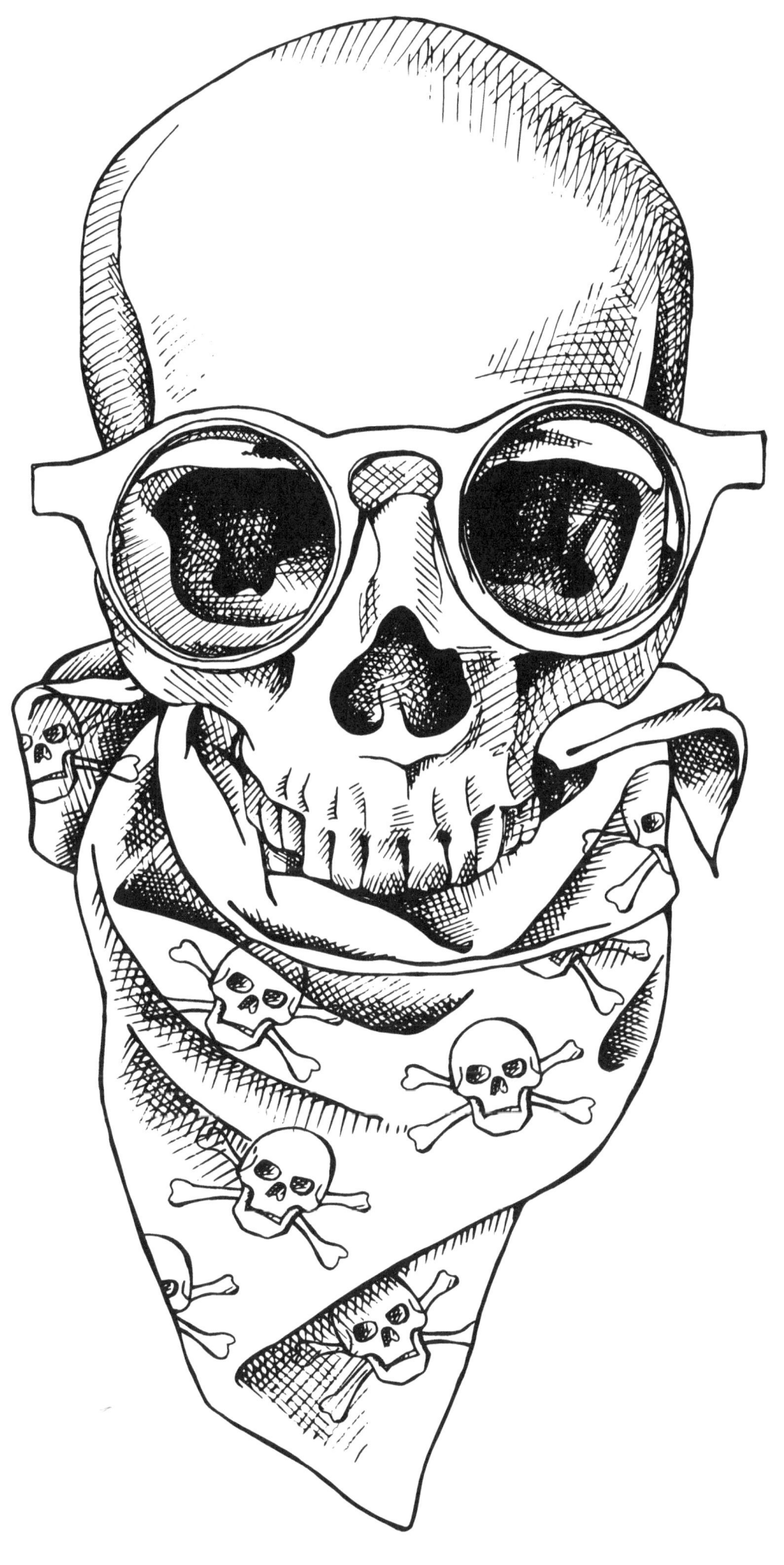

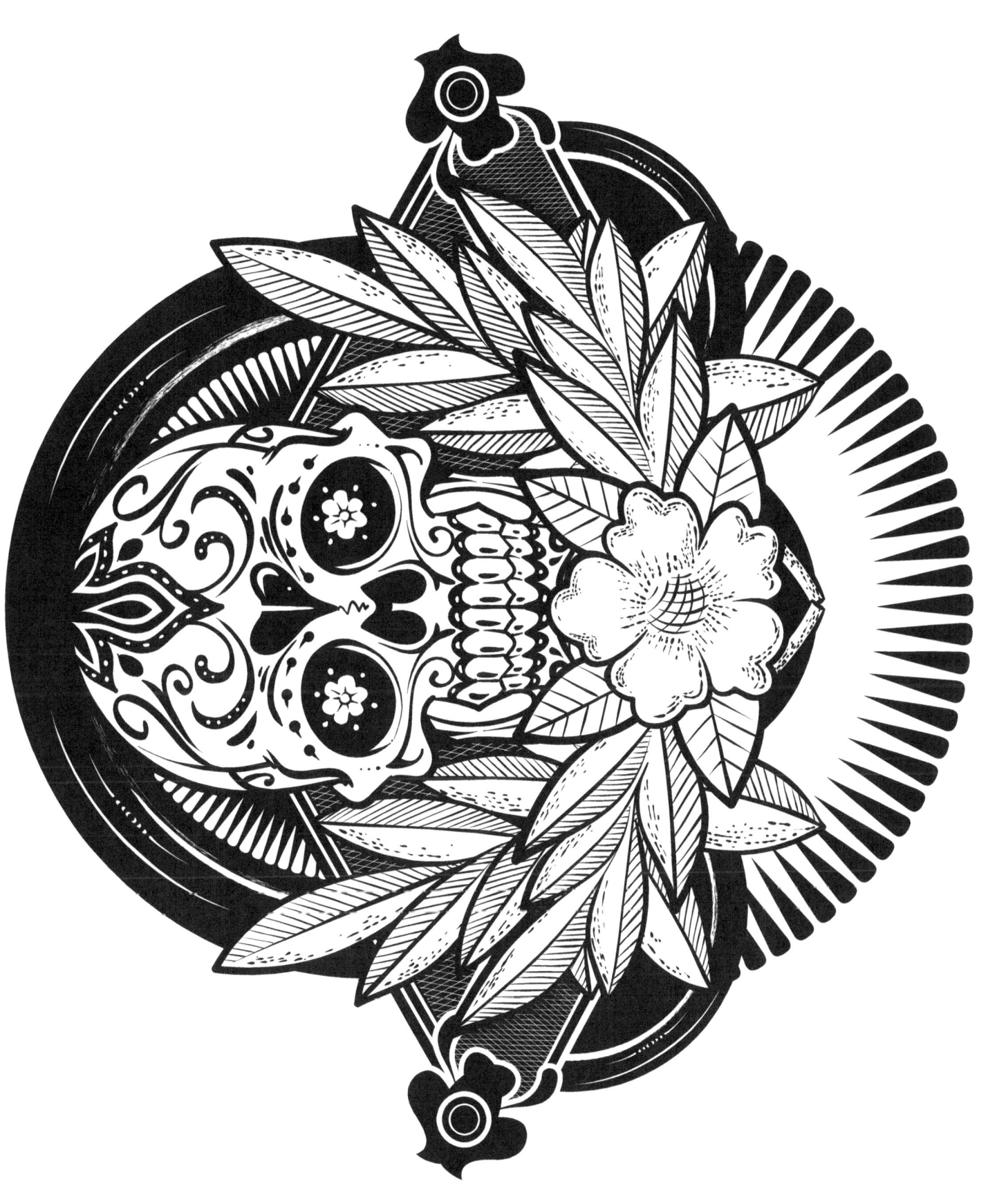

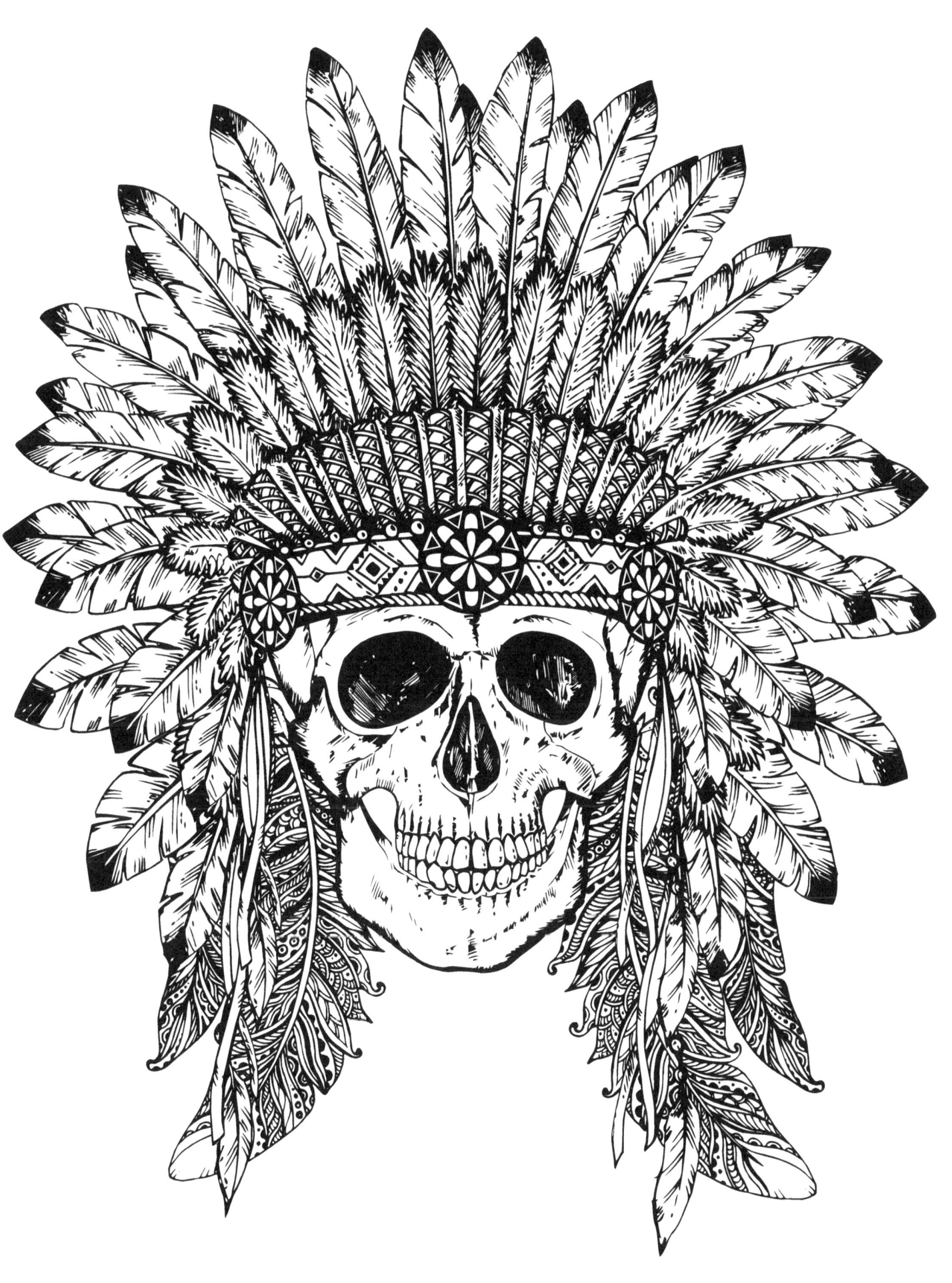

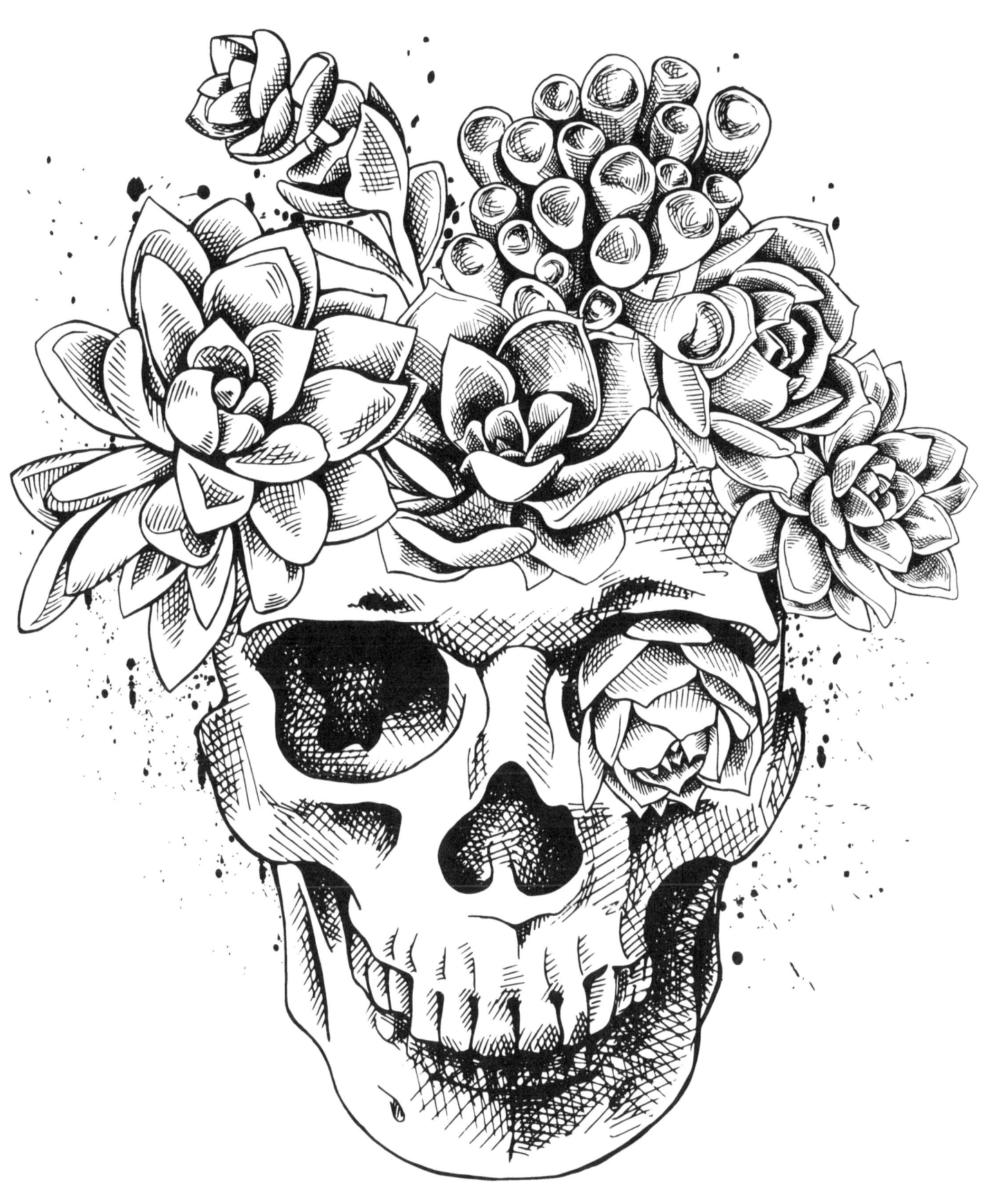

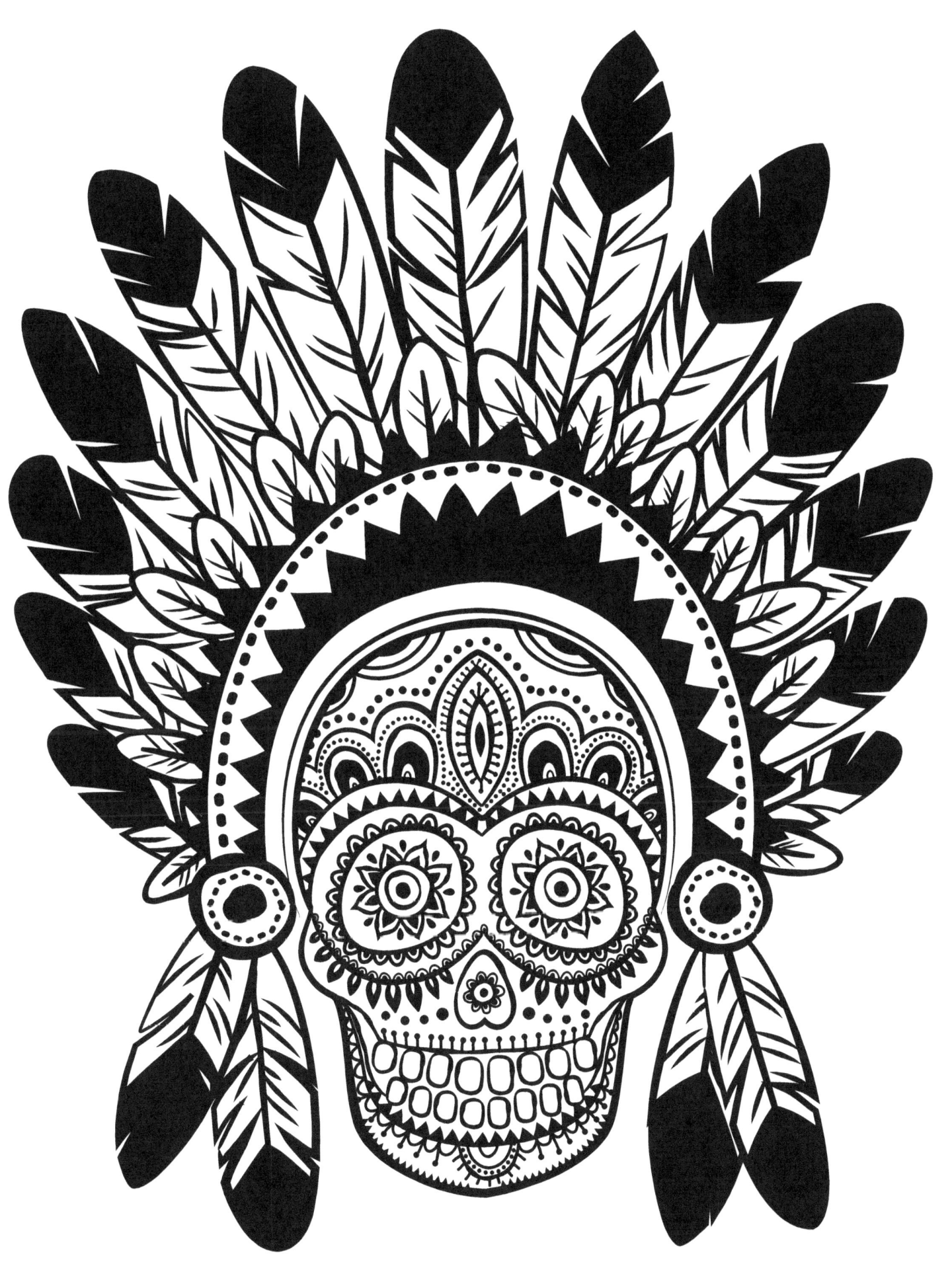

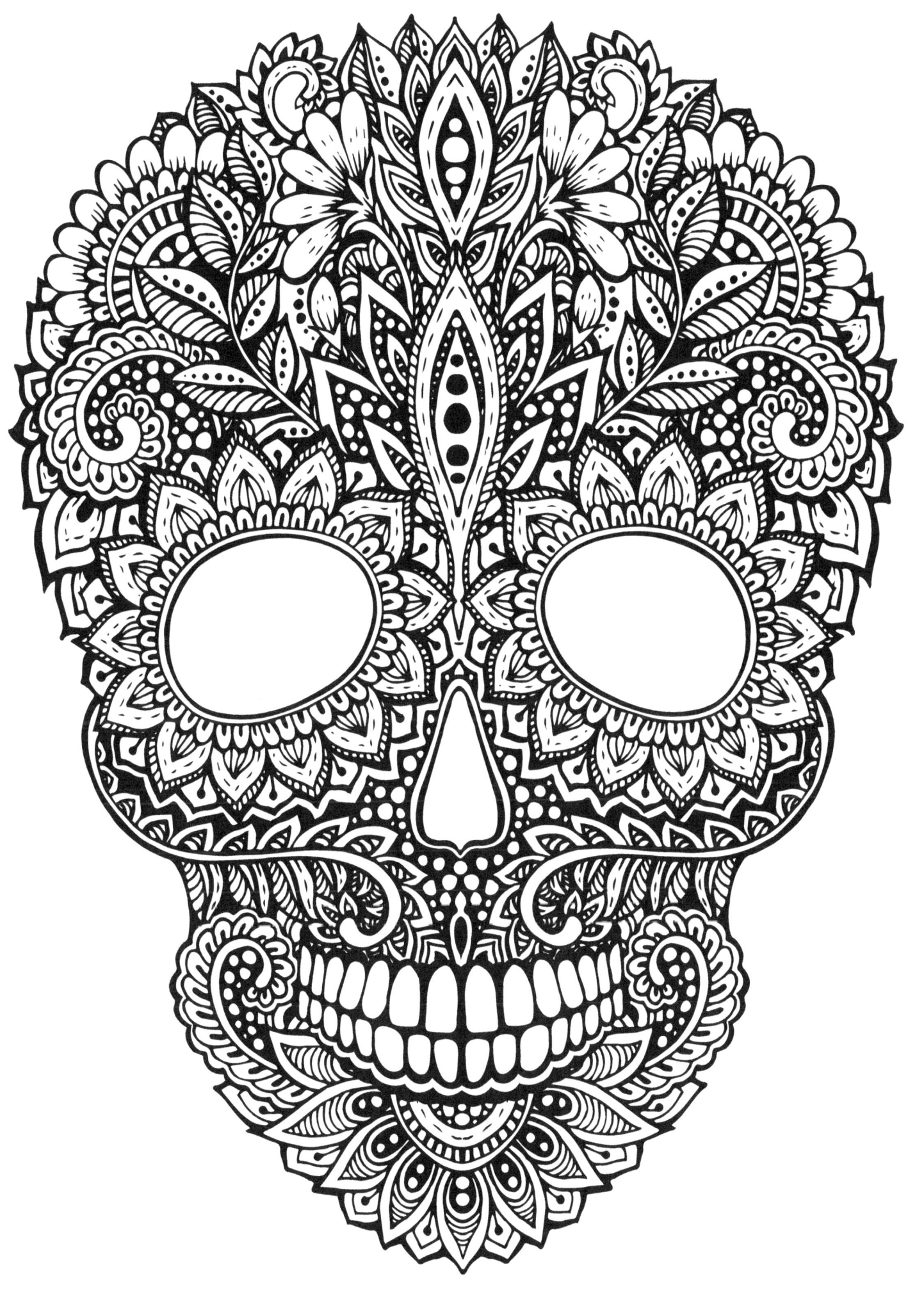

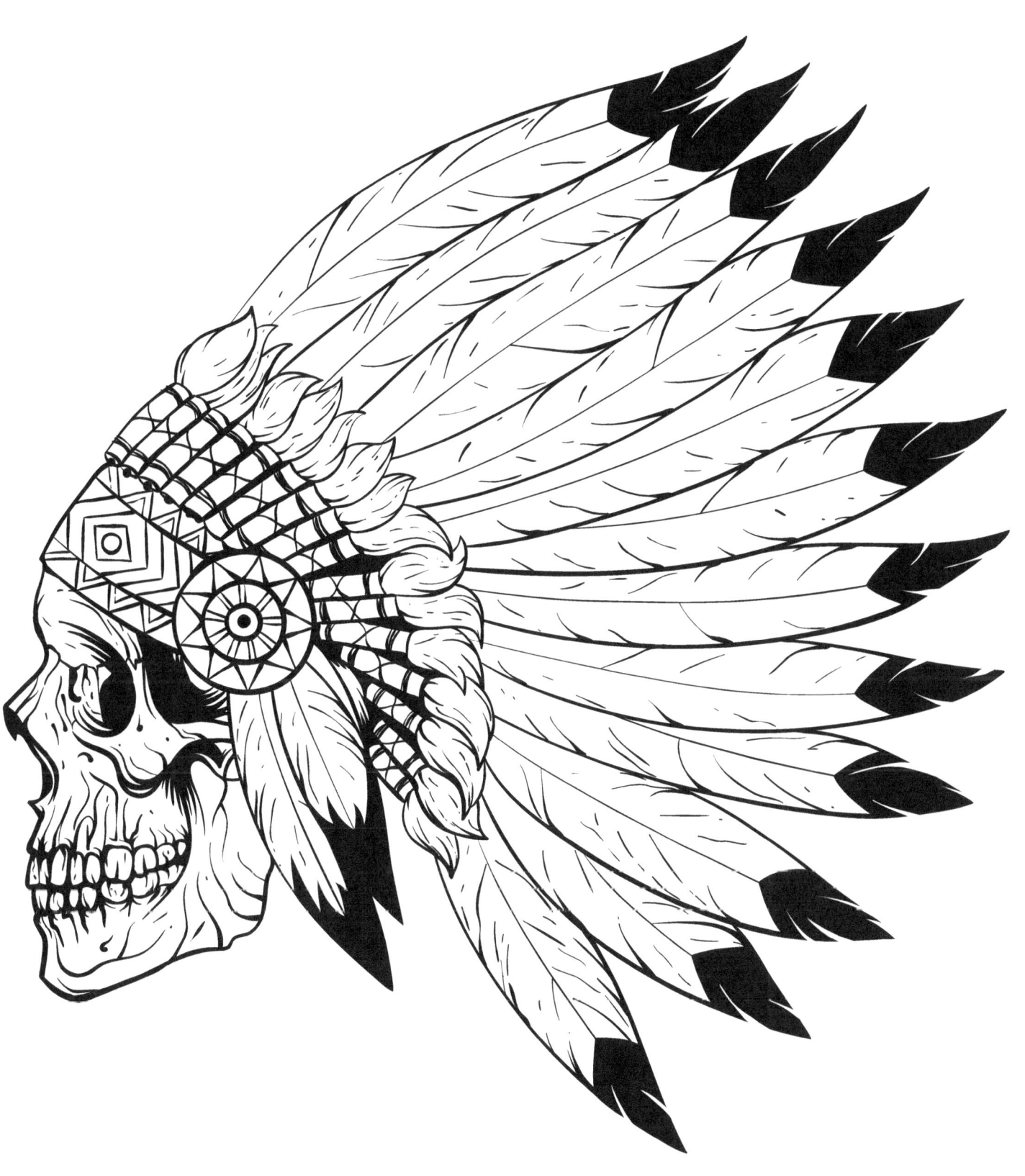

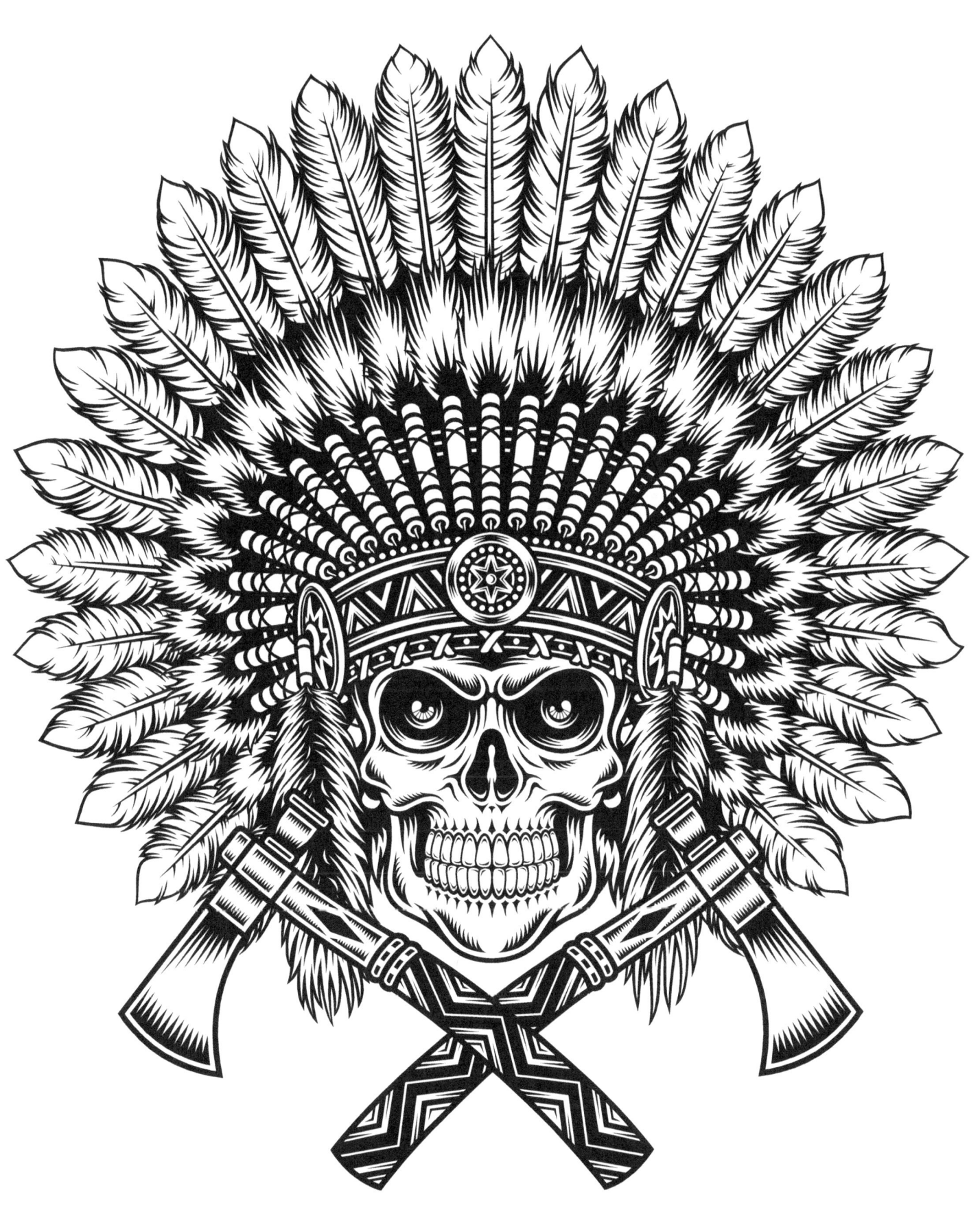

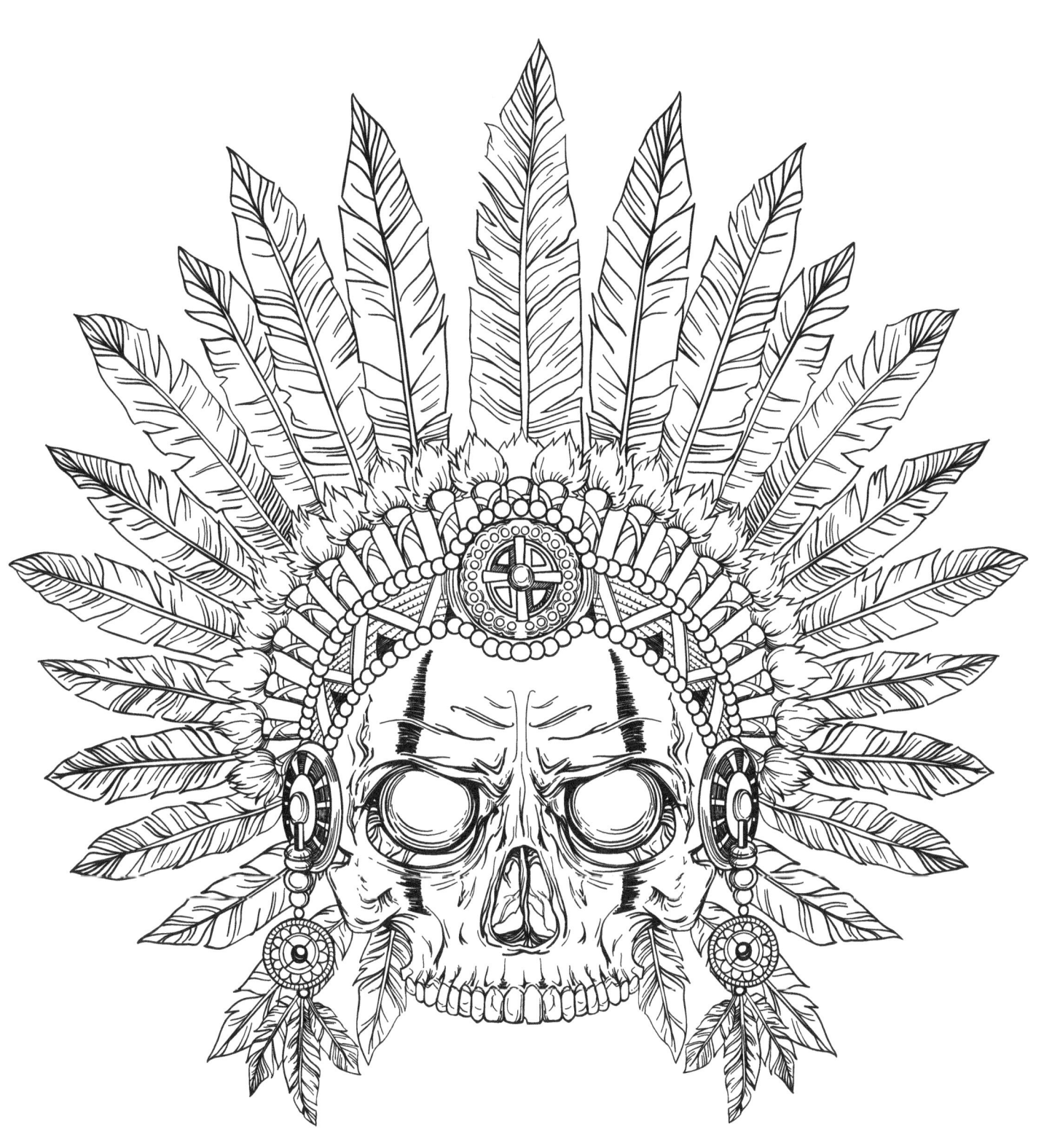

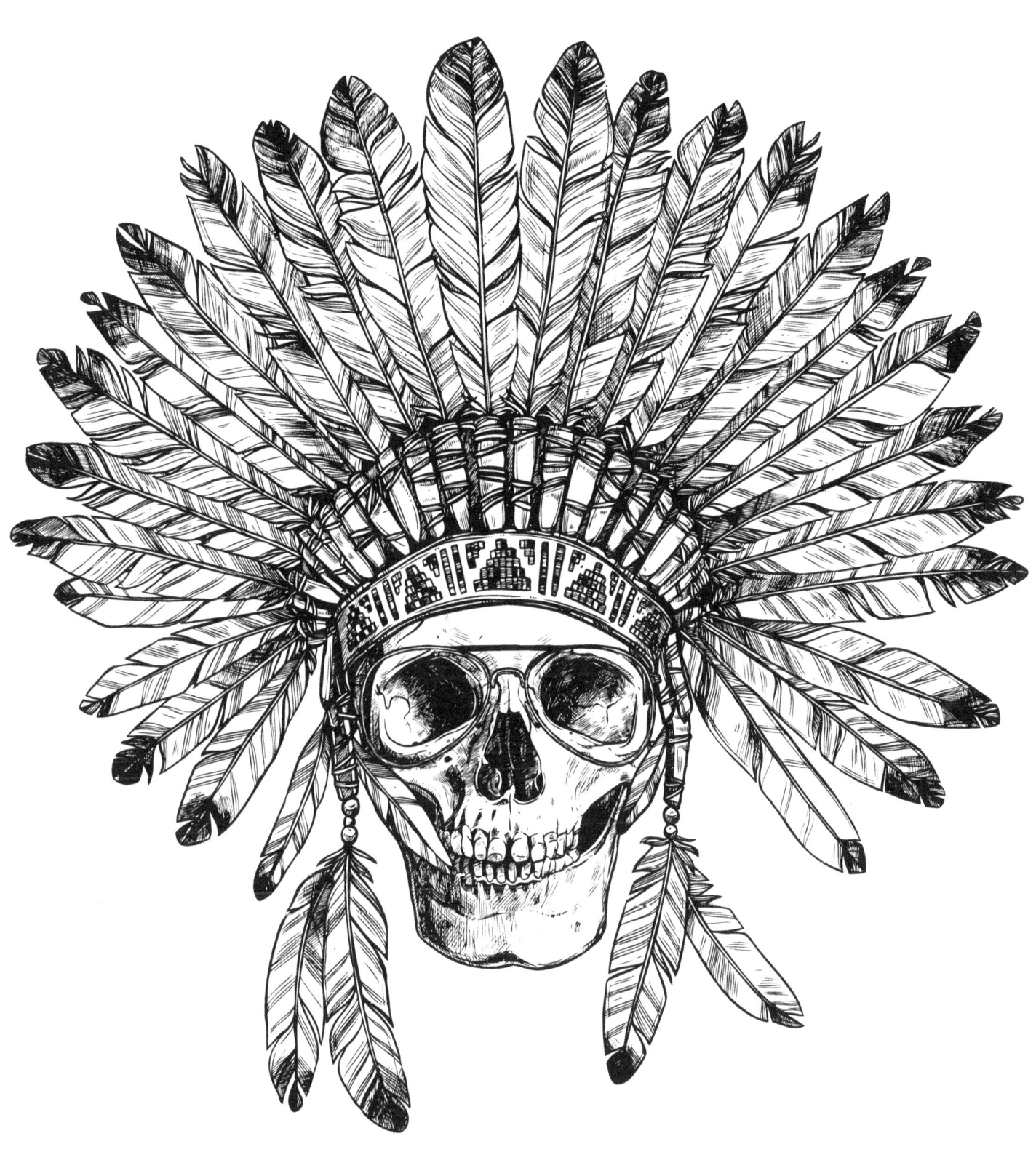

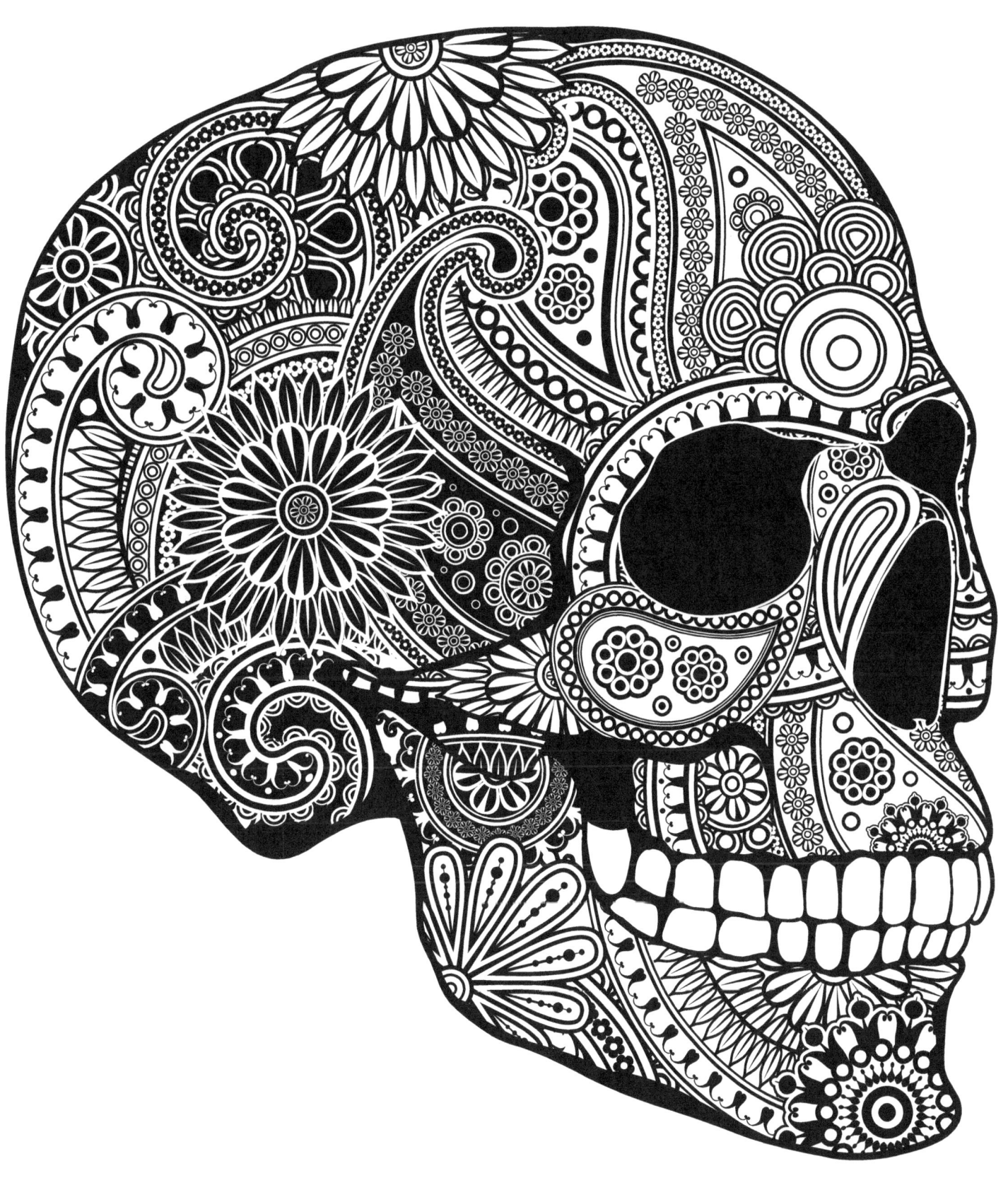

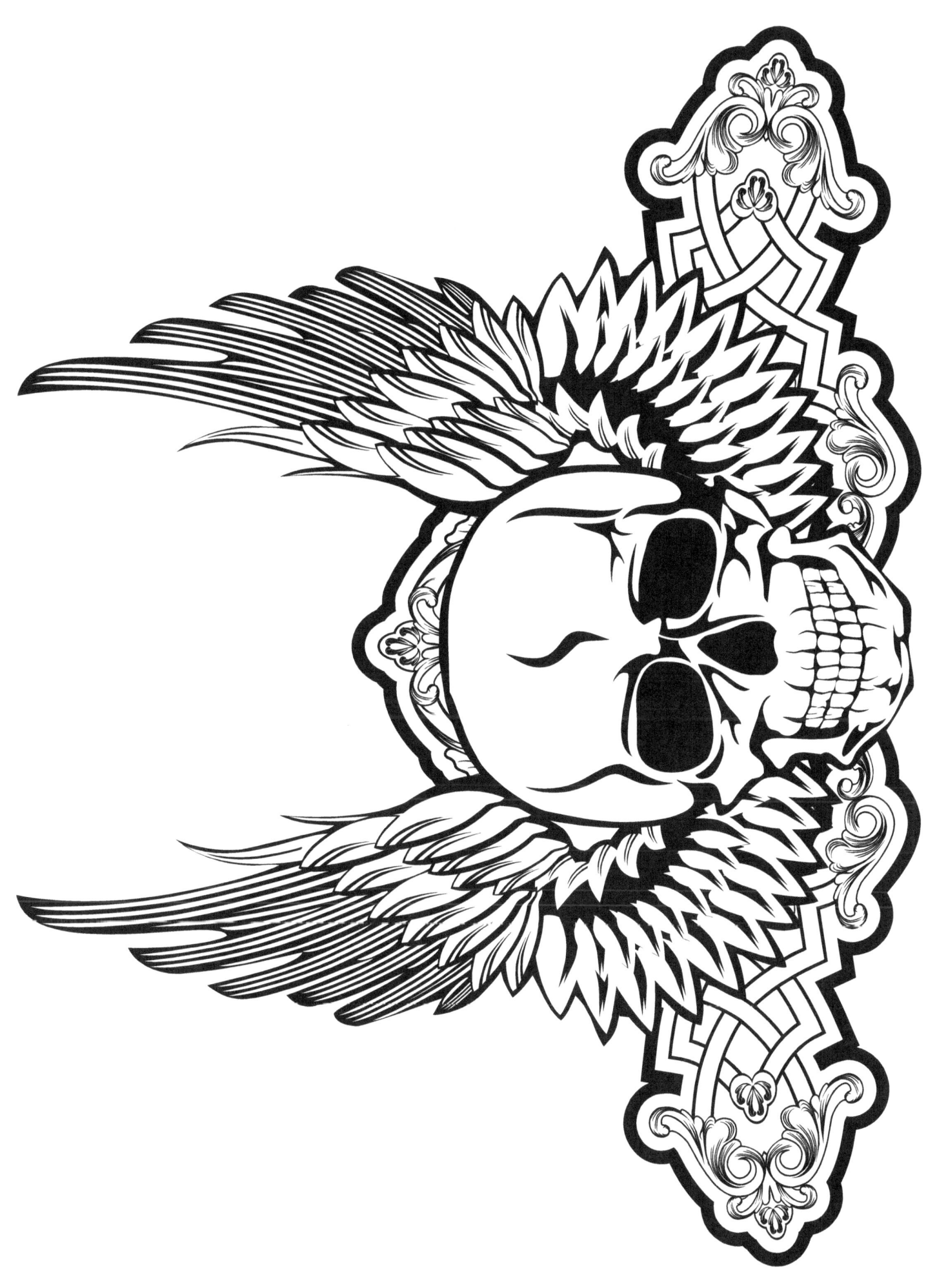

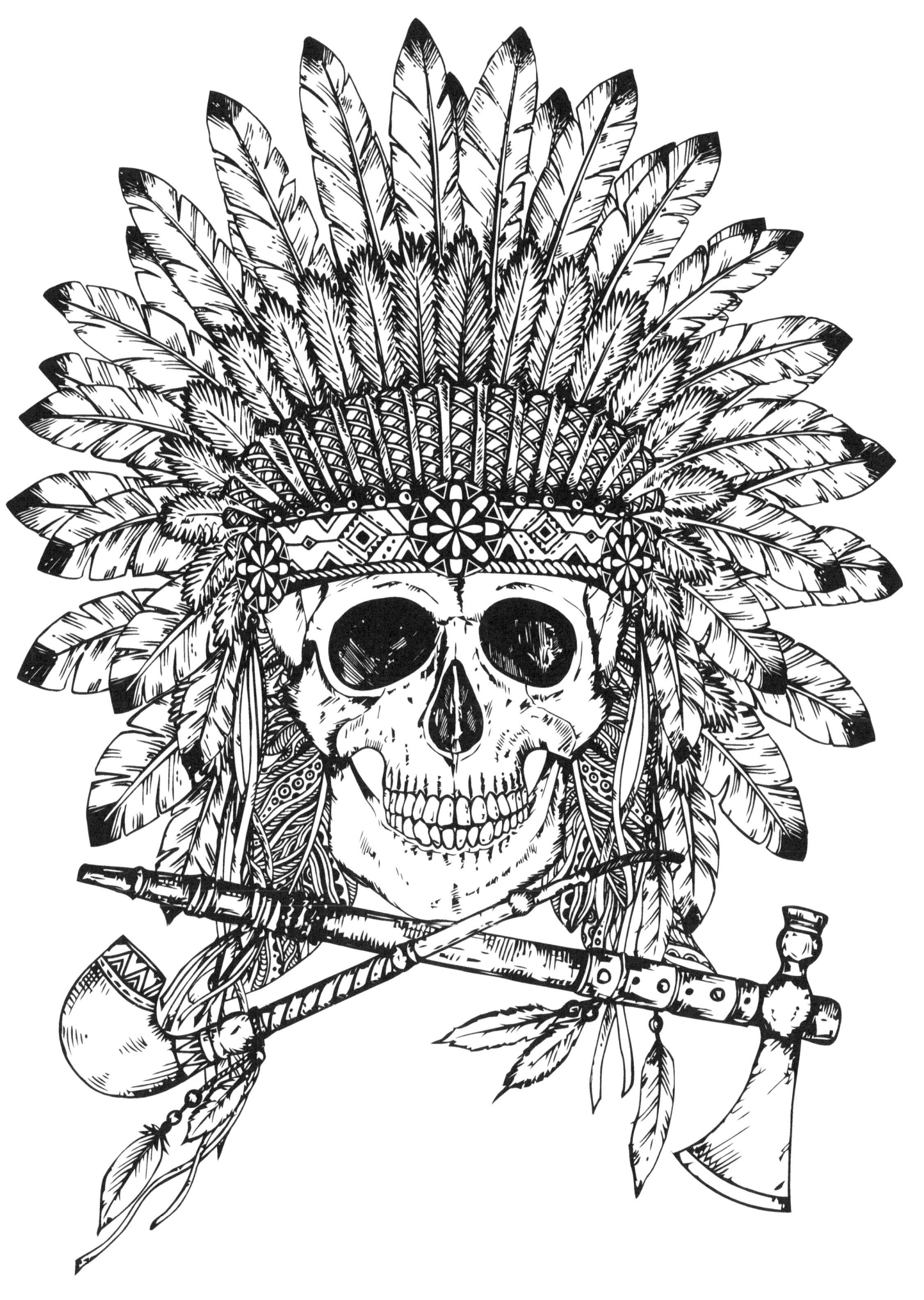

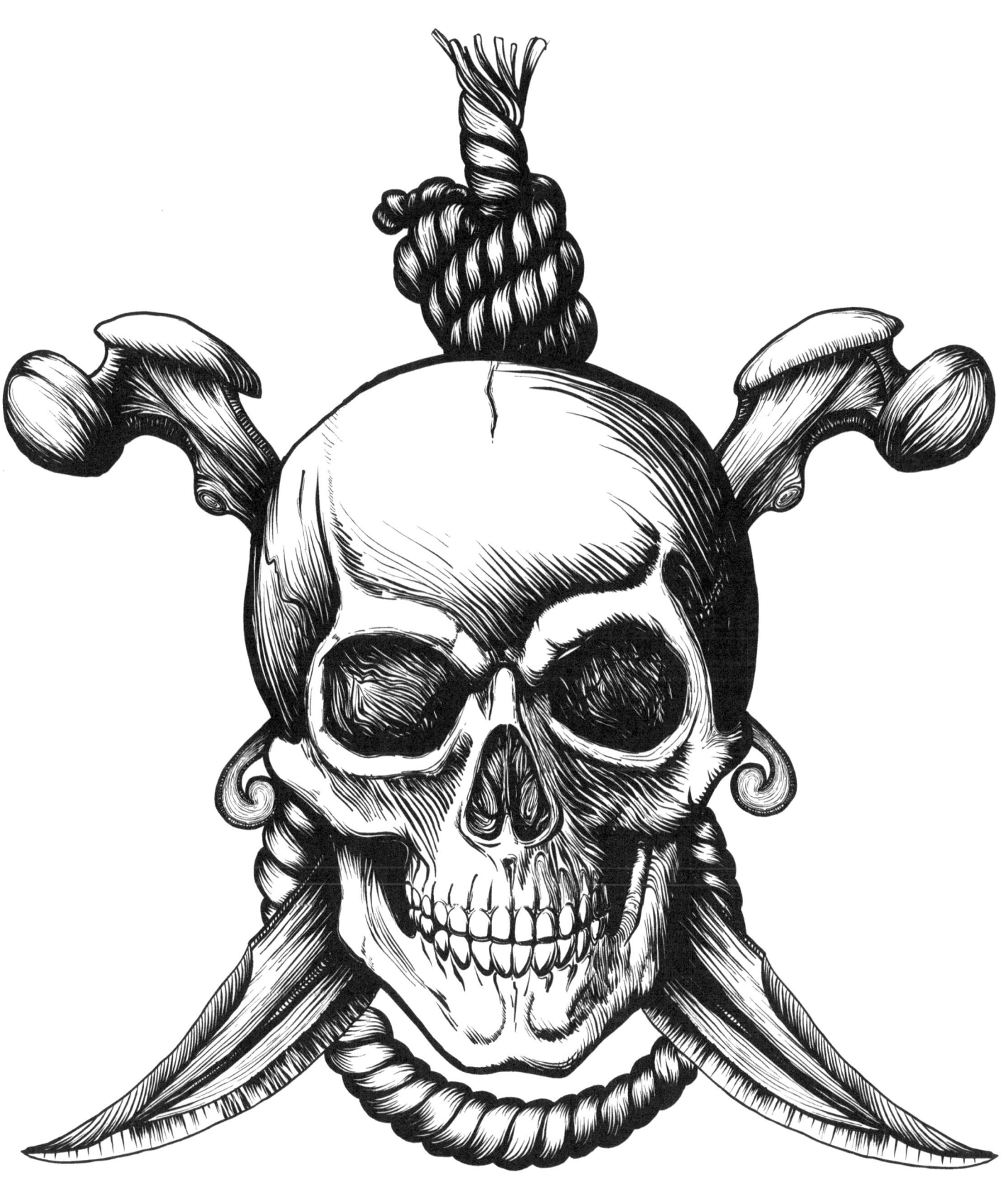

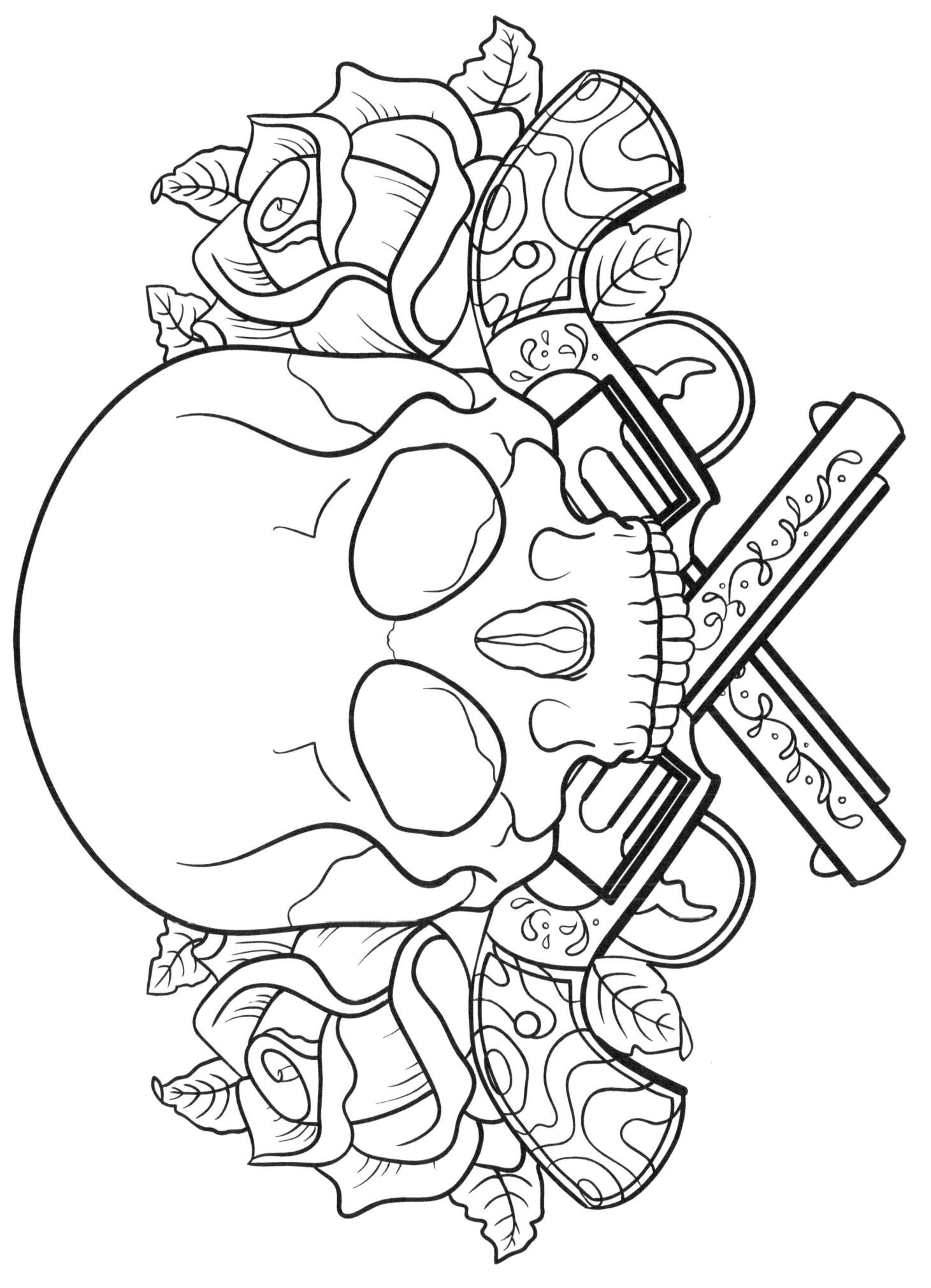

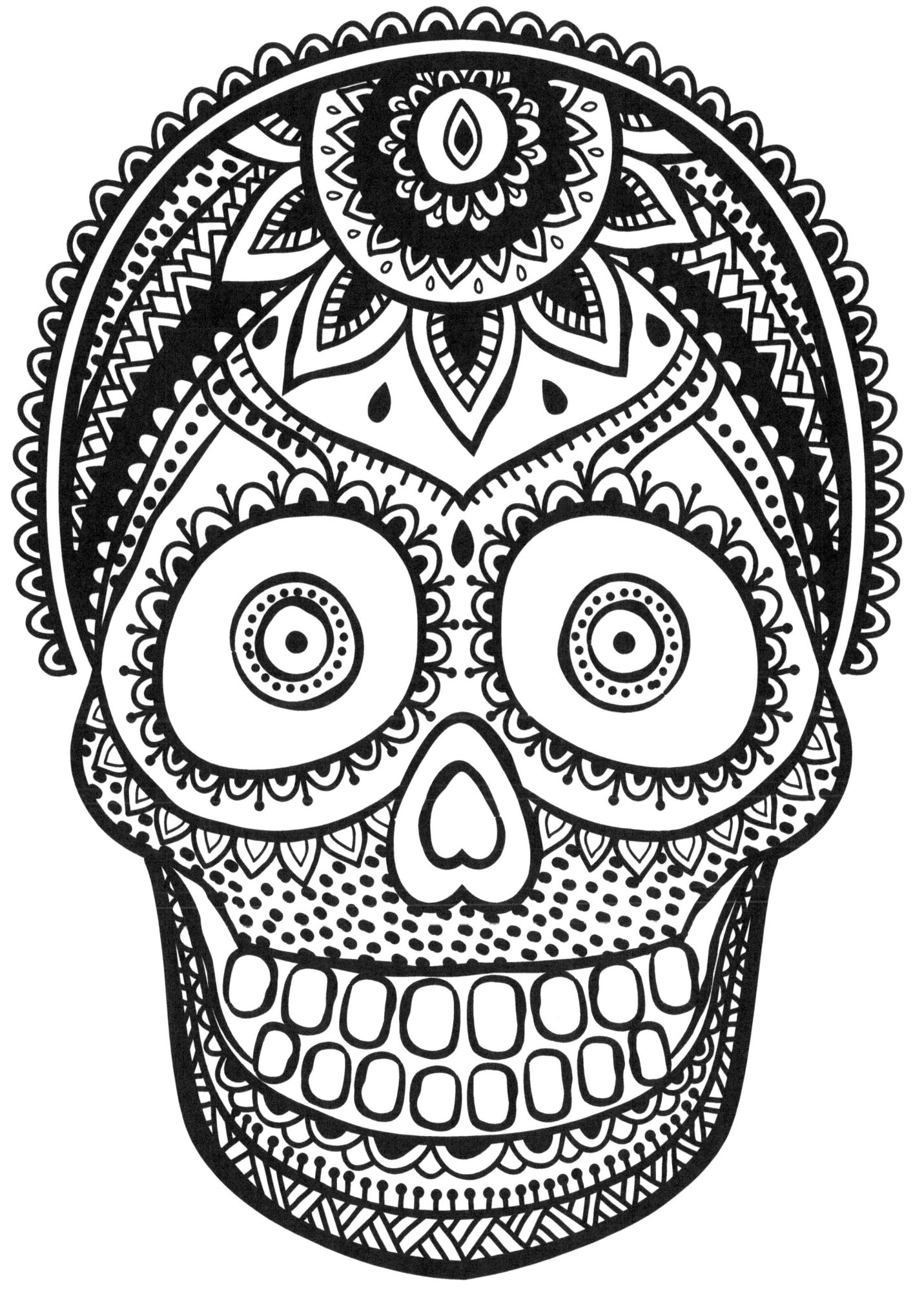

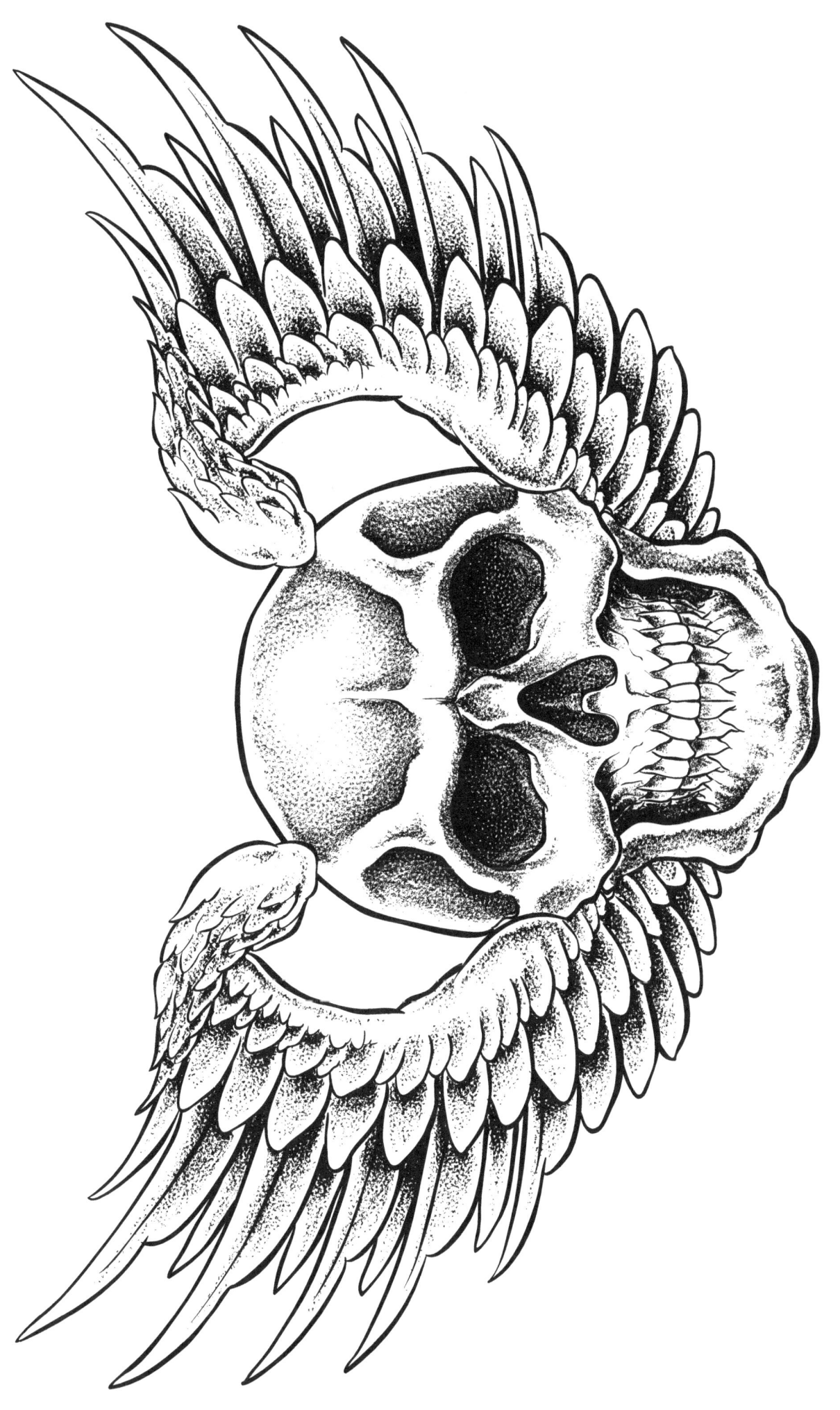

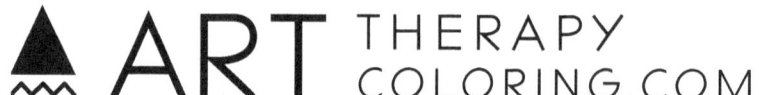

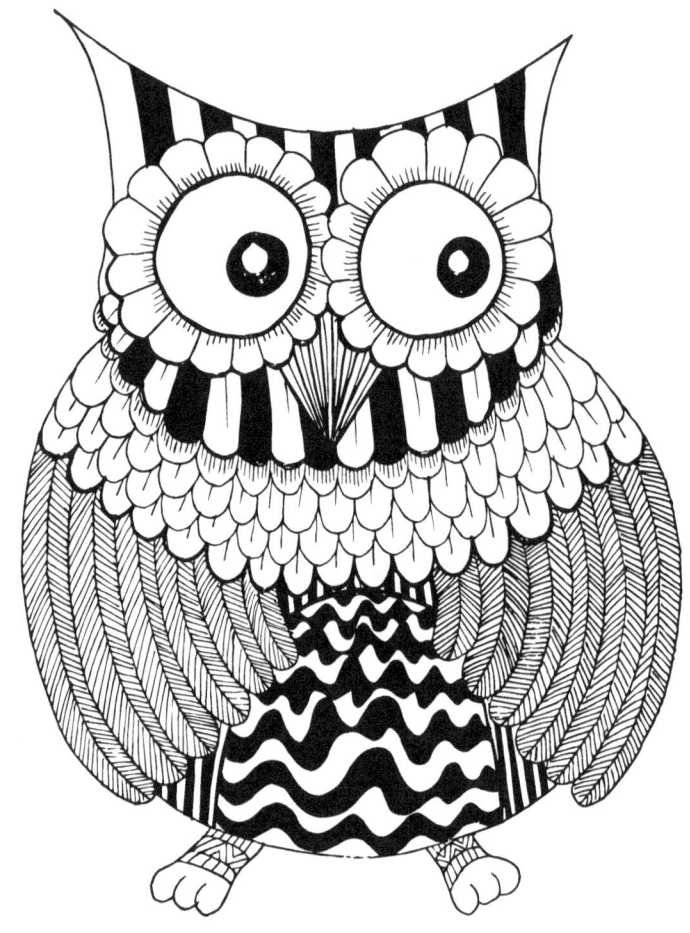

Visit our website at www.arttherapycoloring.com

Get a Free Printable Coloring Ebook!

We've created an exclusive offer for our customers to receive a free Adult Coloring Ebook.

Visit **www.arttherapycoloring.com/freebie** to claim your free coloring book with over 30 new designs that you can instantly print and color!

Over 100 Art Therapy Coloring Books

See our collection of over 100 Art Therapy Coloring Books for Adults, Men, Seniors, Teens, Kids, Boys, and Girls on the following pages.

Coloring Books For Adults

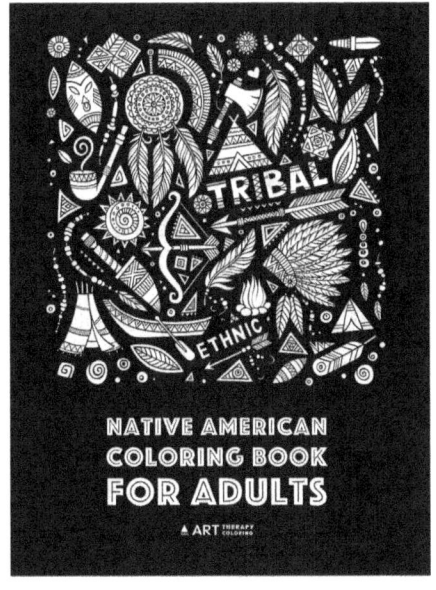

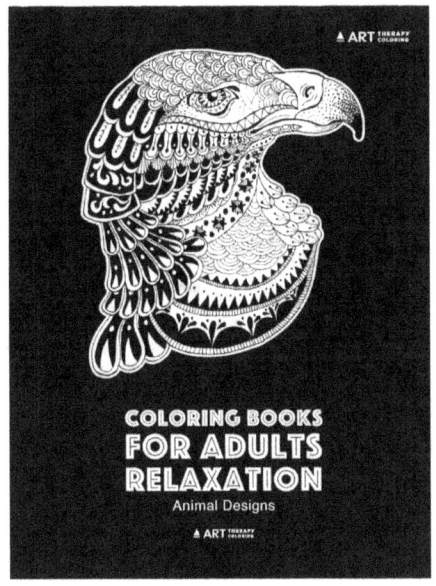

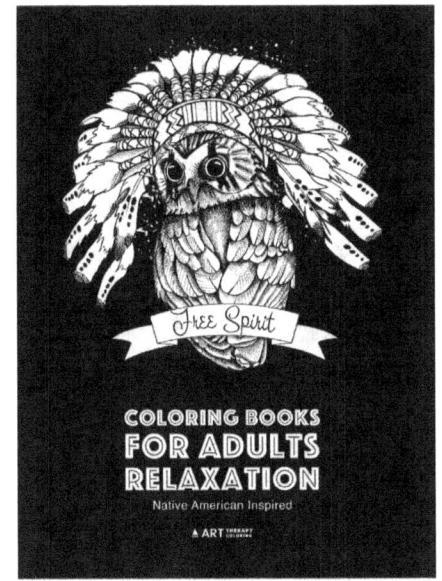

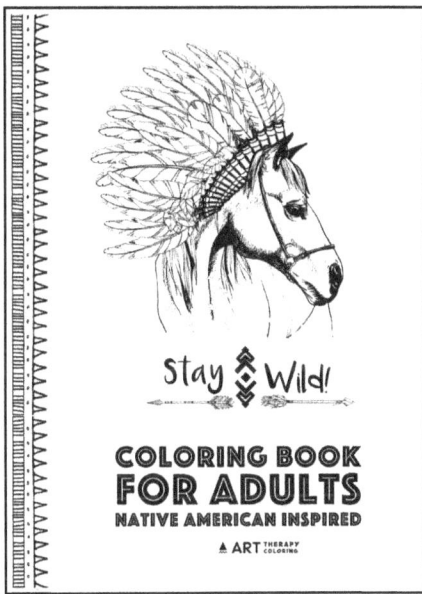

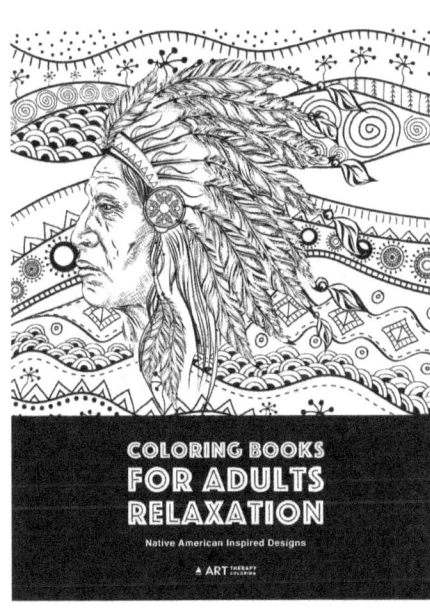

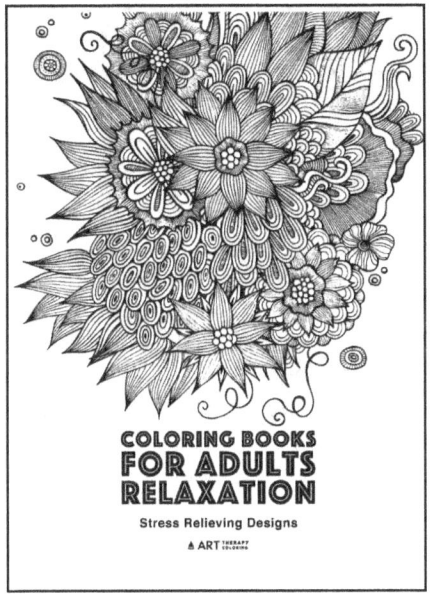

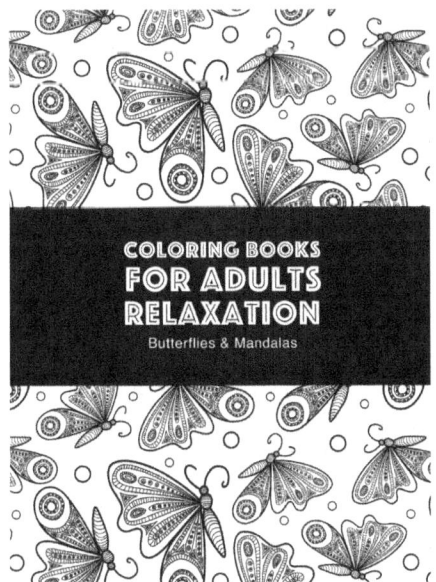

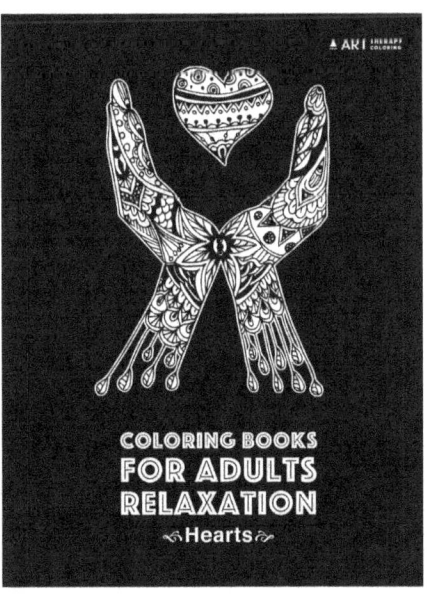

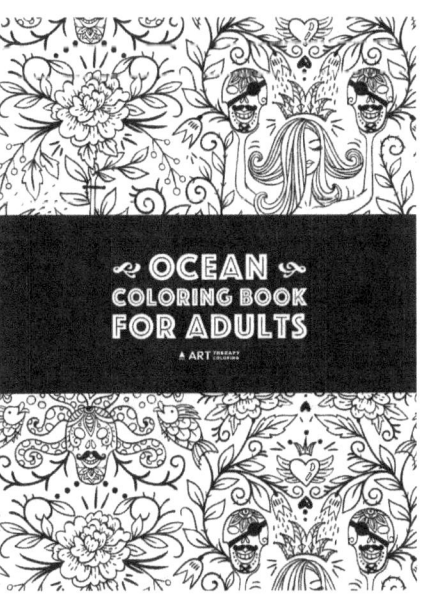

Coloring Books For Adults

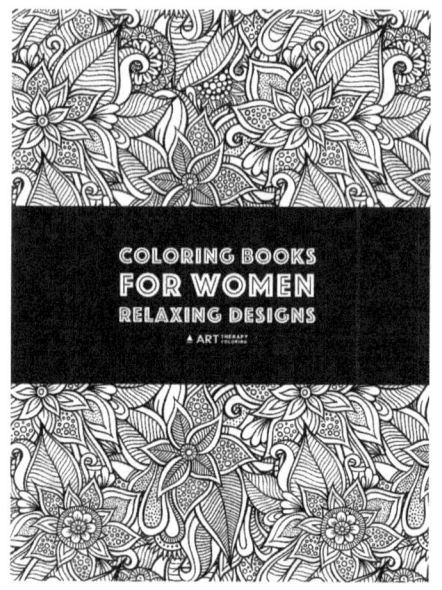

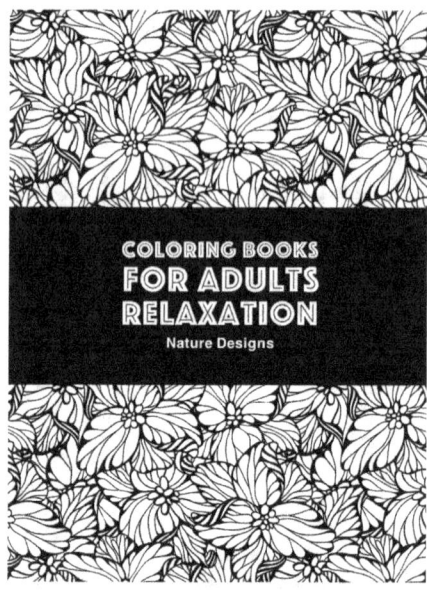

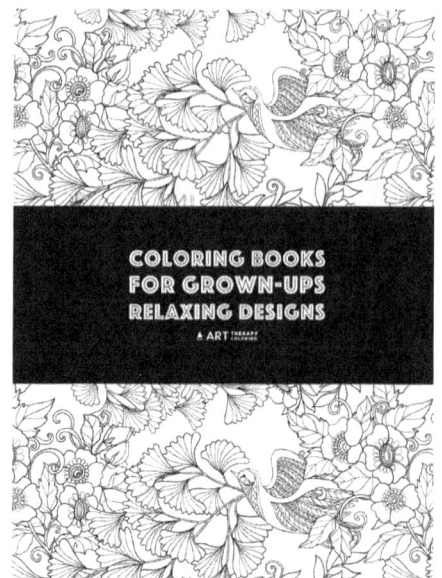

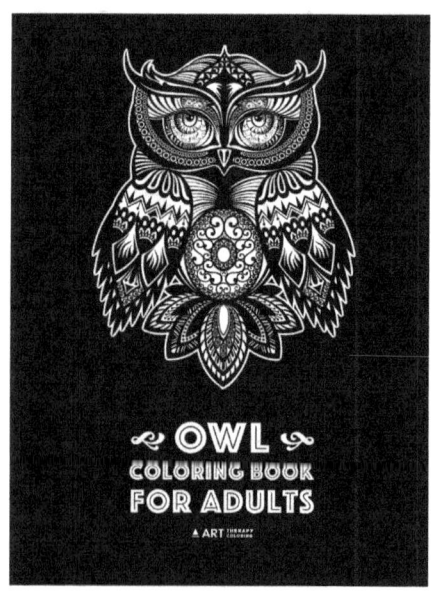

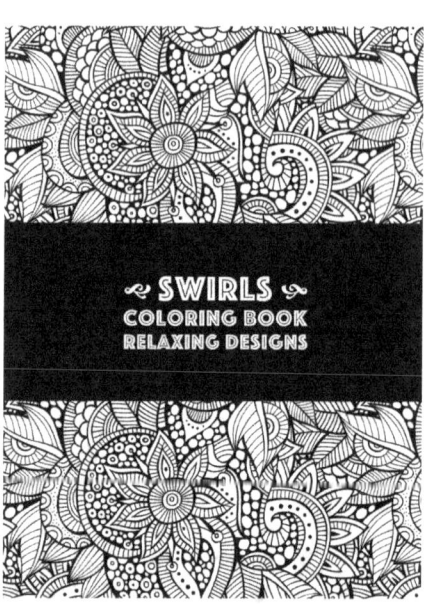

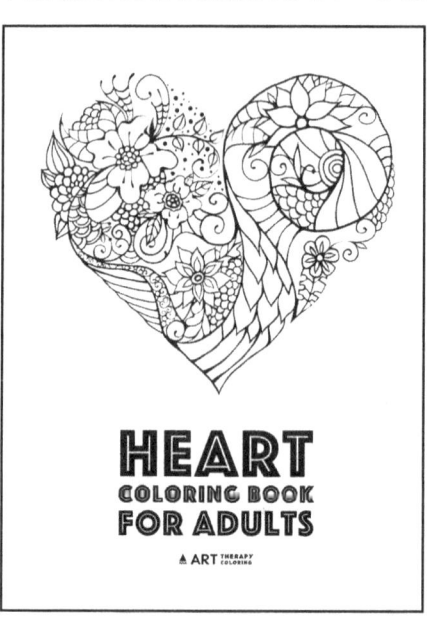

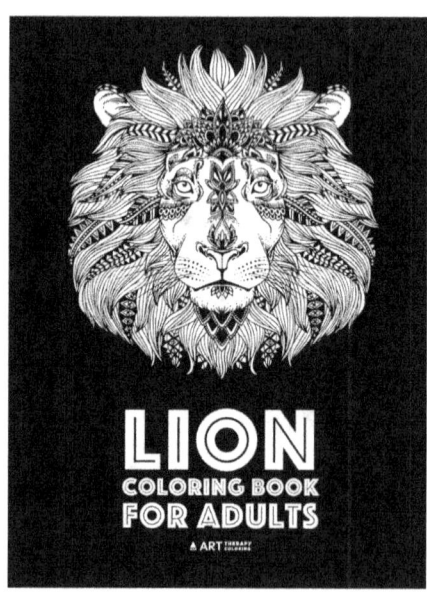

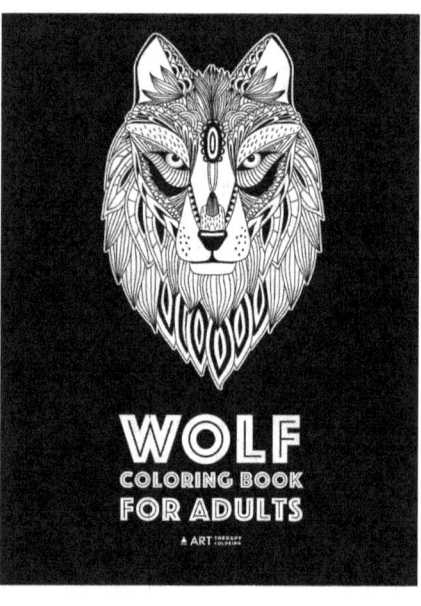

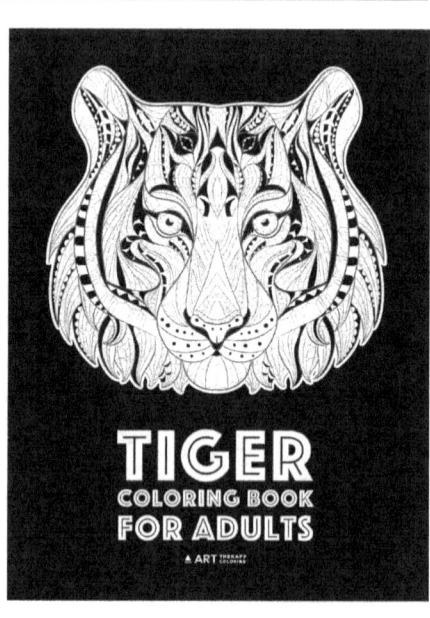

Coloring Books For Men

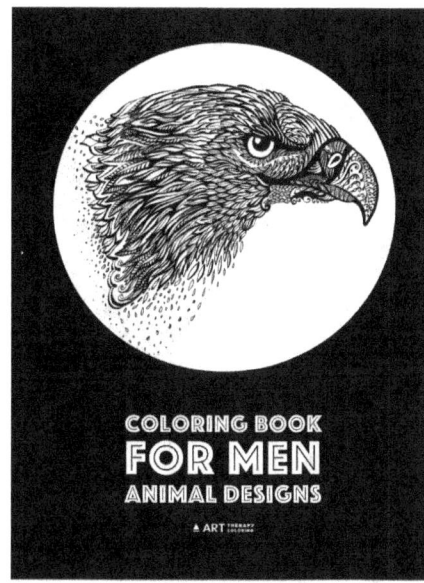

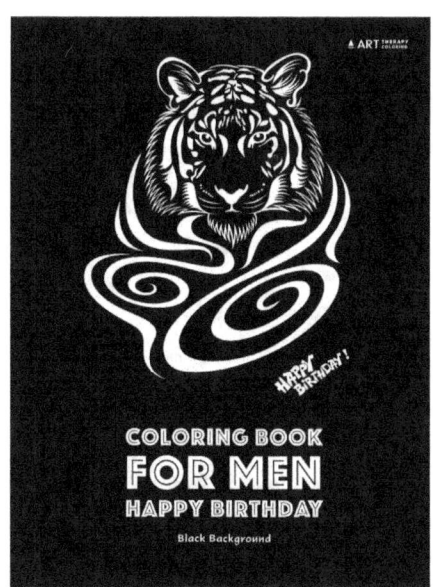

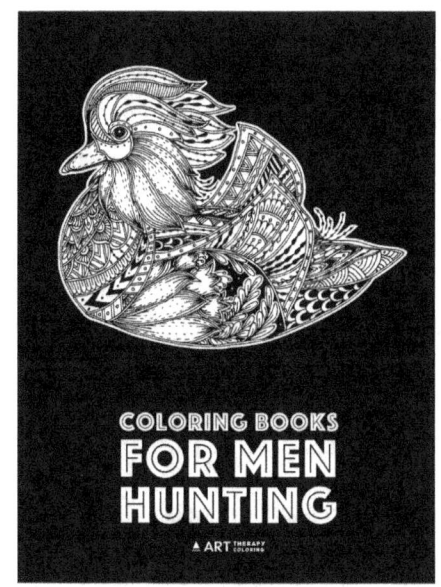

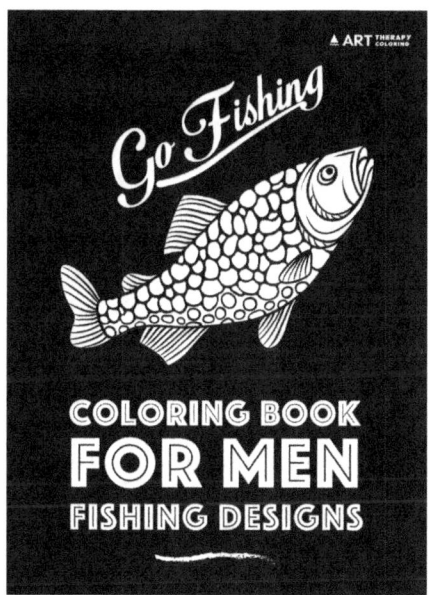

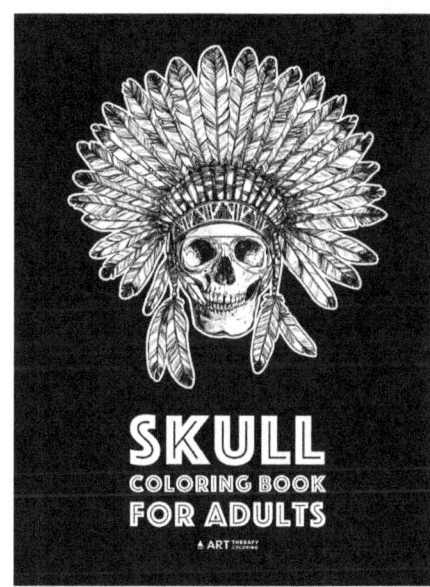

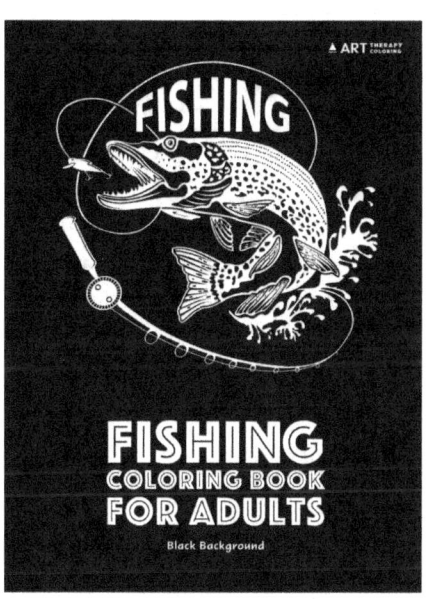

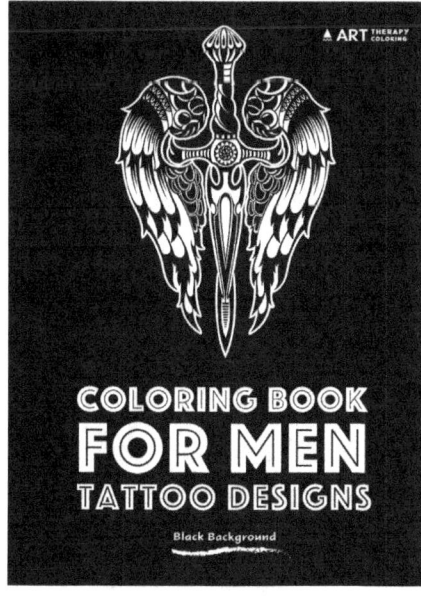

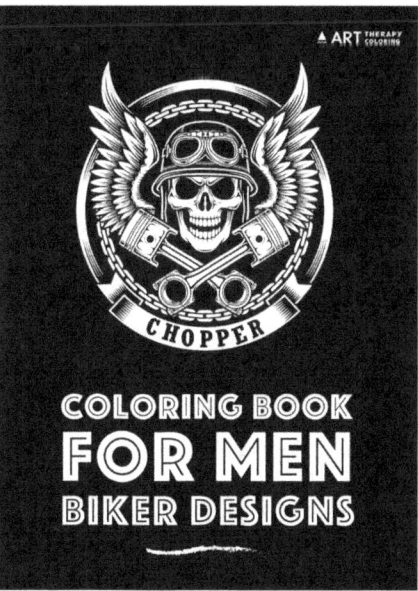

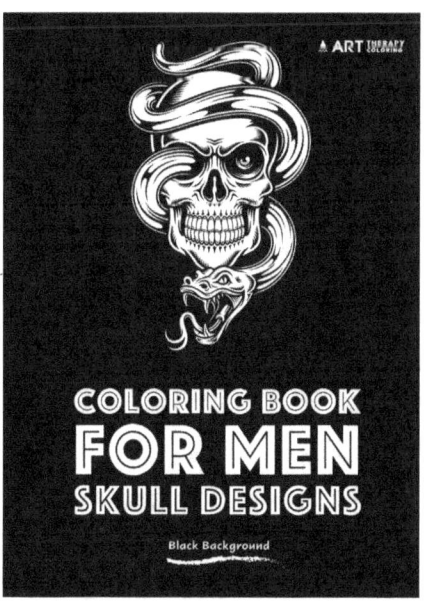

Coloring Books For Seniors

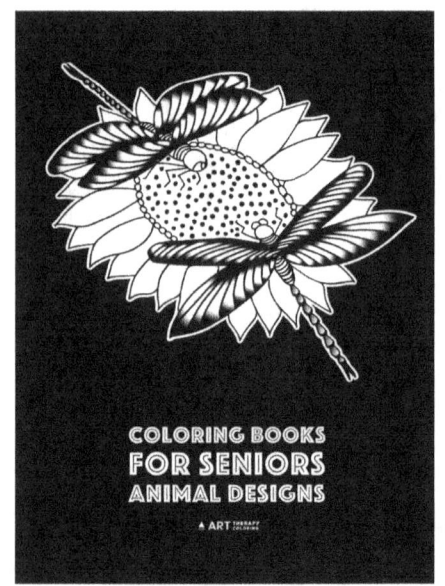

COLORING BOOKS
FOR SENIORS
ANIMAL DESIGNS
ART THERAPY COLORING

COLORING BOOKS
FOR SENIORS
SWIRL DESIGNS
Black Background

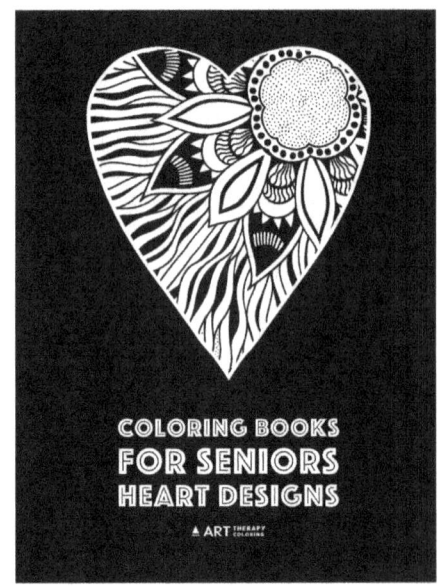

COLORING BOOKS
FOR SENIORS
HEART DESIGNS
ART THERAPY COLORING

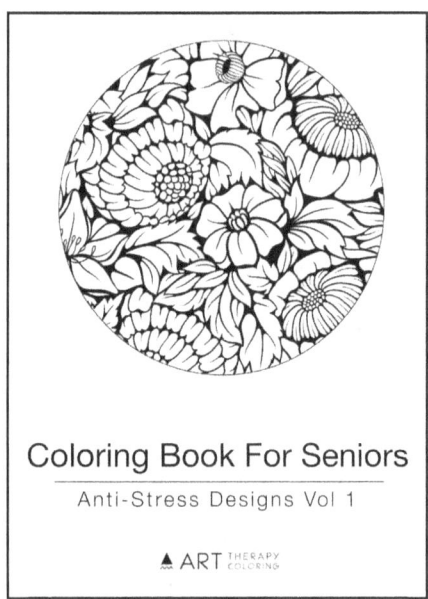

Coloring Book For Seniors

Anti-Stress Designs Vol 1

ART THERAPY COLORING

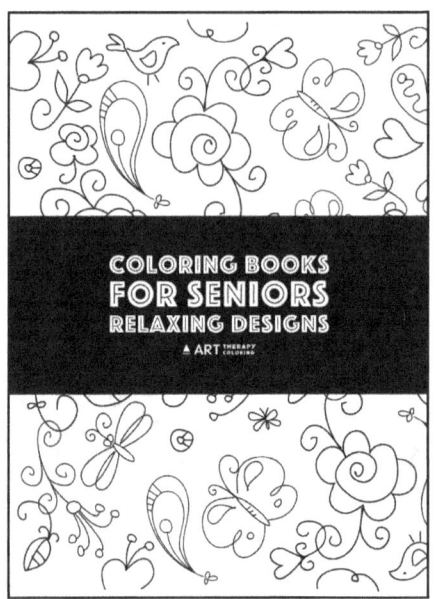

COLORING BOOKS
FOR SENIORS
RELAXING DESIGNS
ART THERAPY COLORING

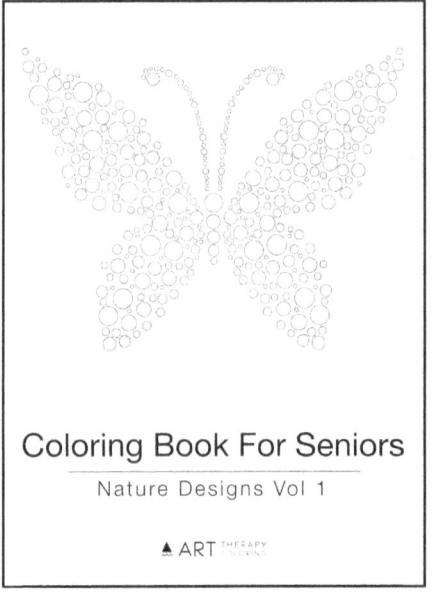

Coloring Book For Seniors

Nature Designs Vol 1

ART THERAPY COLORING

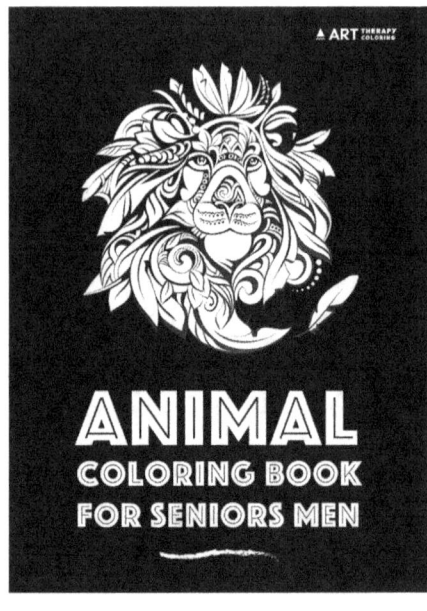

ANIMAL
COLORING BOOK
FOR SENIORS MEN

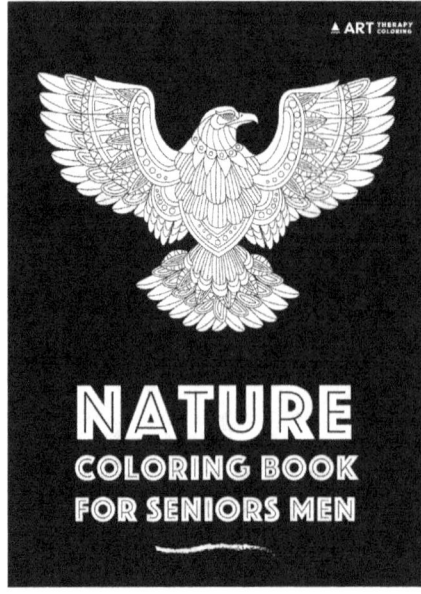

NATURE
COLORING BOOK
FOR SENIORS MEN

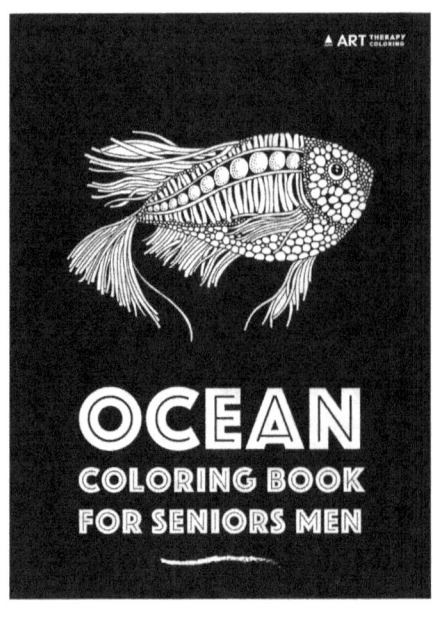

OCEAN
COLORING BOOK
FOR SENIORS MEN

Coloring Books For Girls

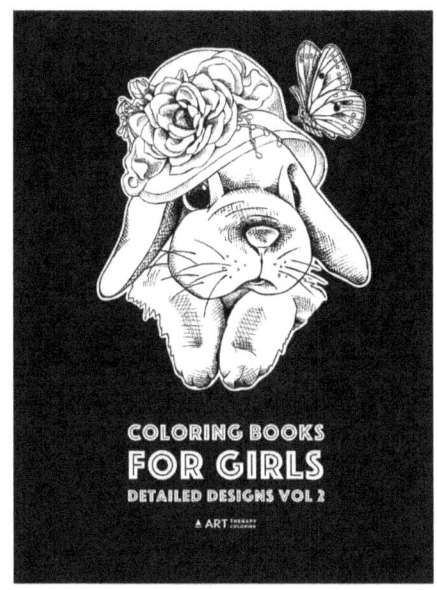

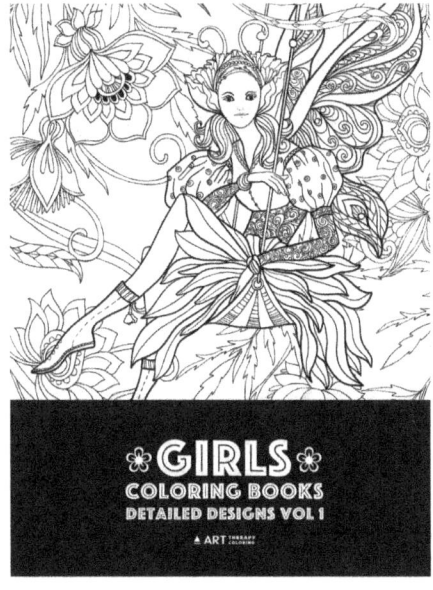

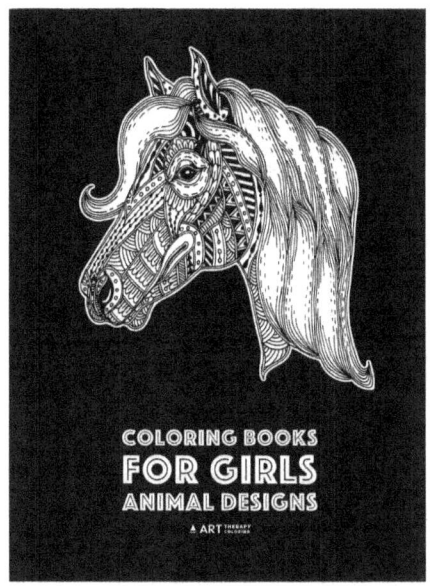

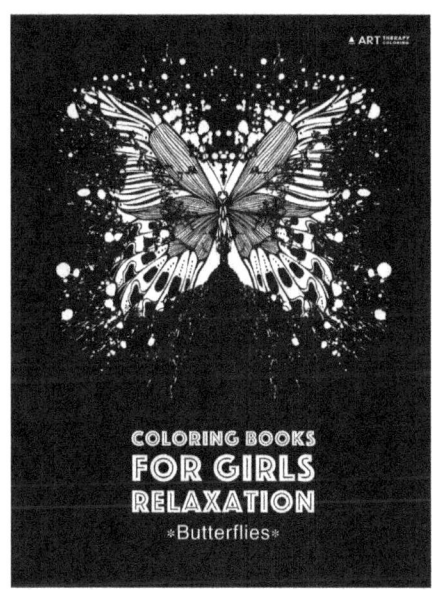

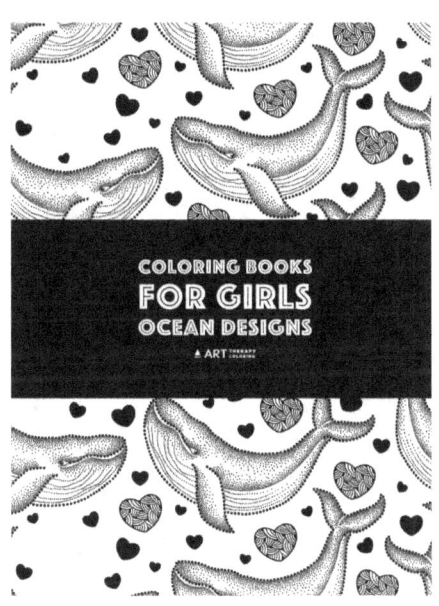

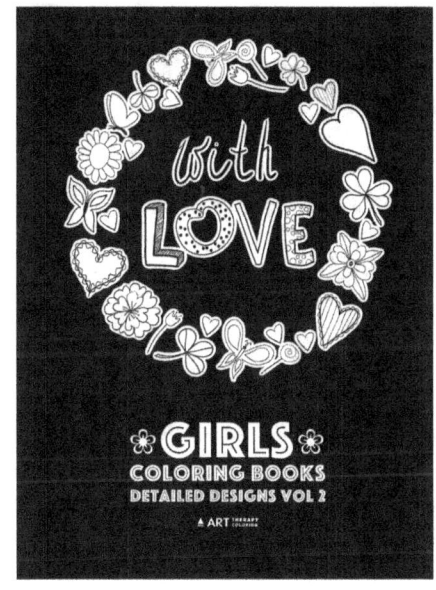

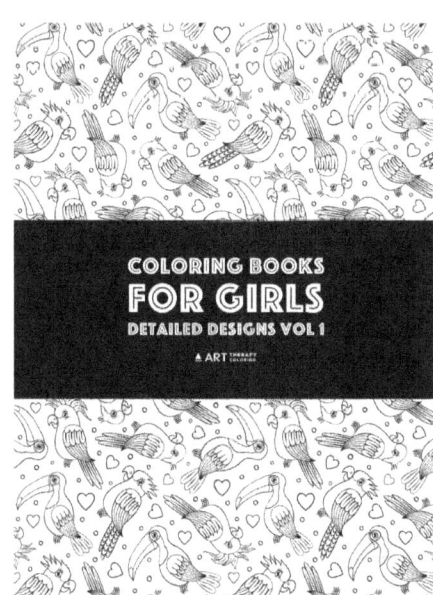

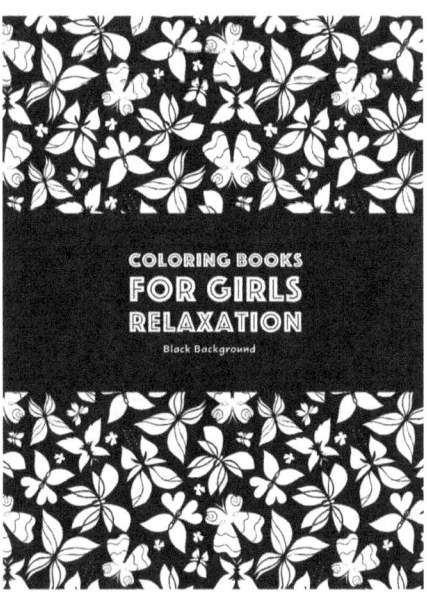

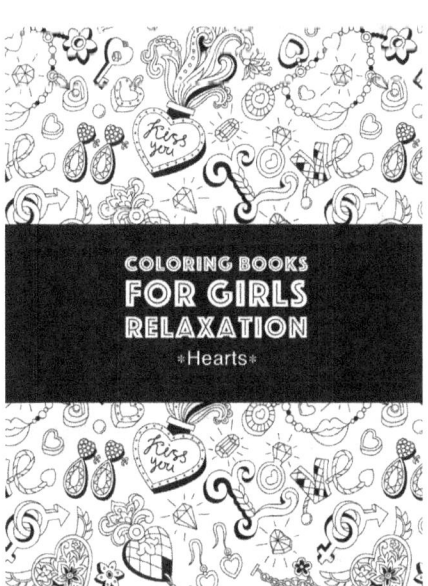

Coloring Books For Boys

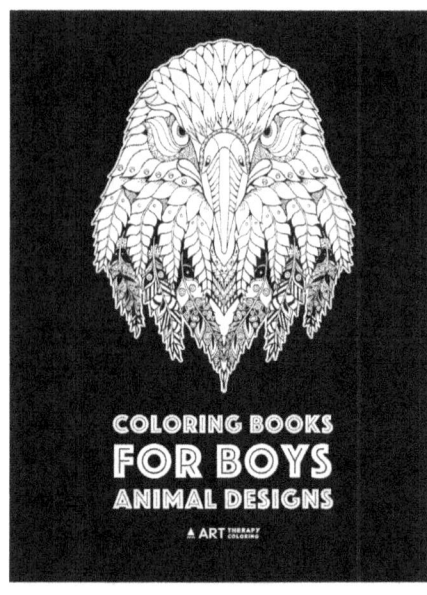

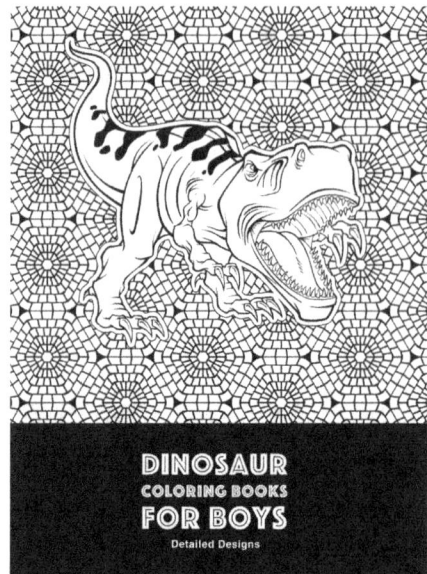

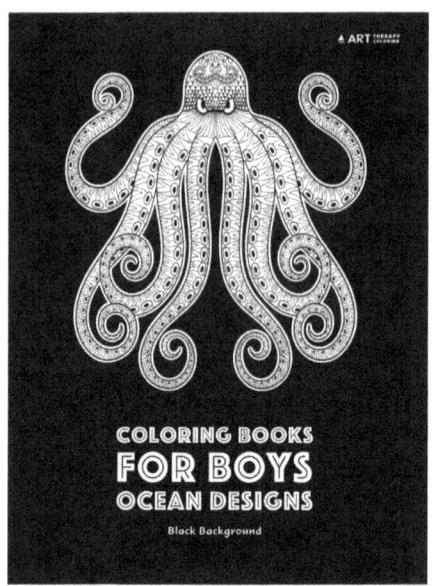

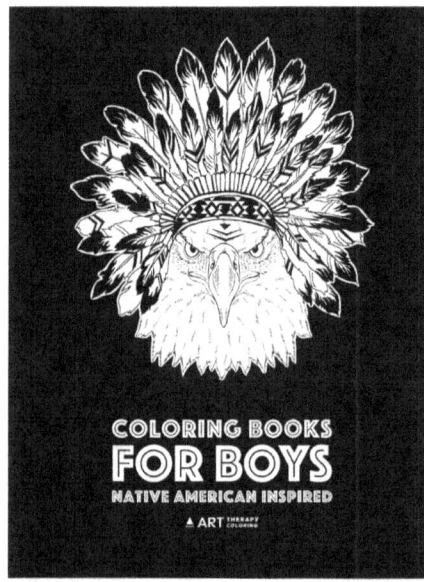

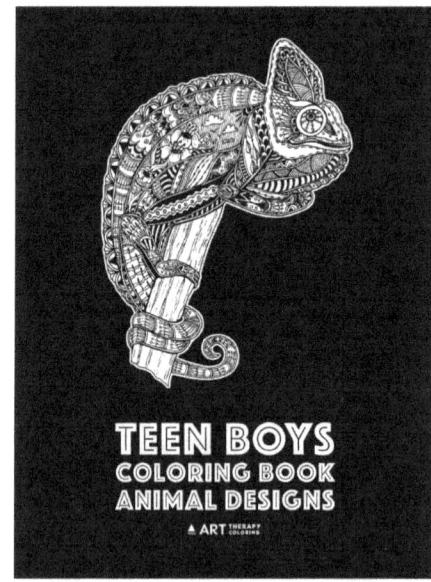

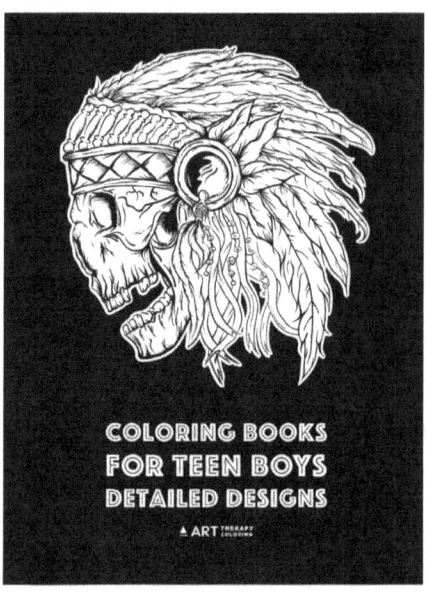

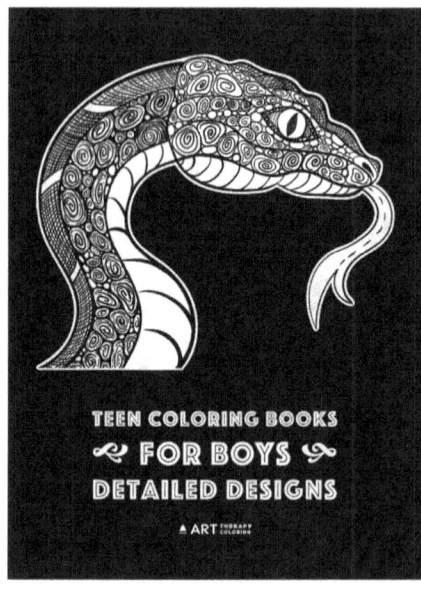

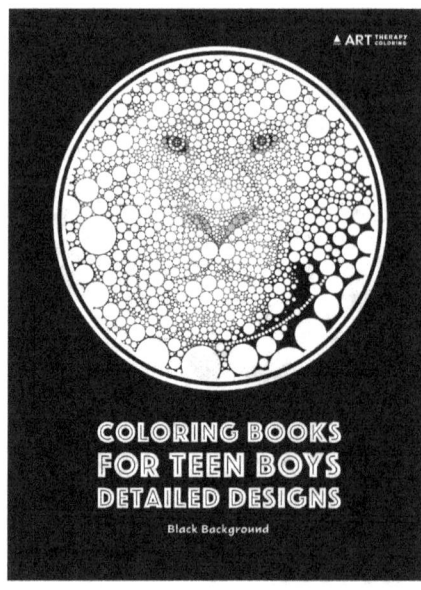

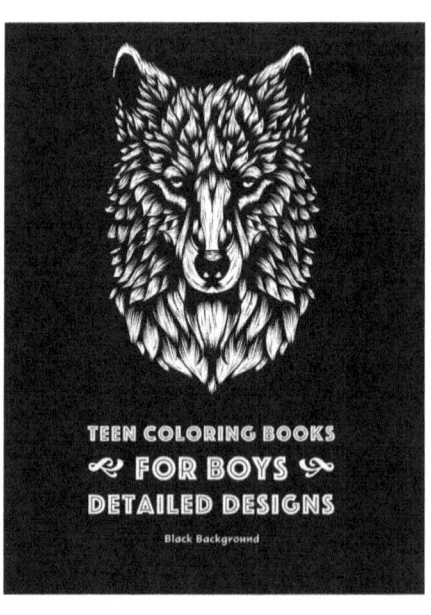

Coloring Books For Kids

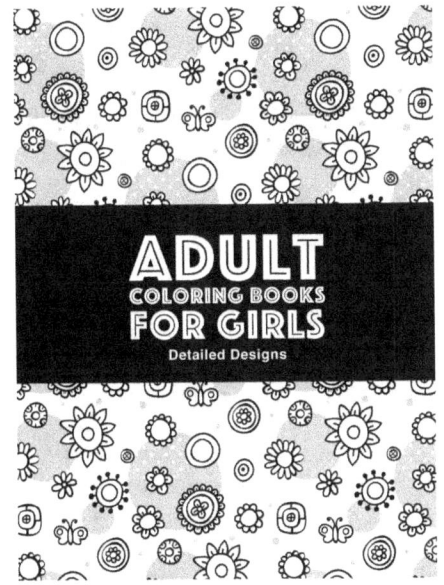

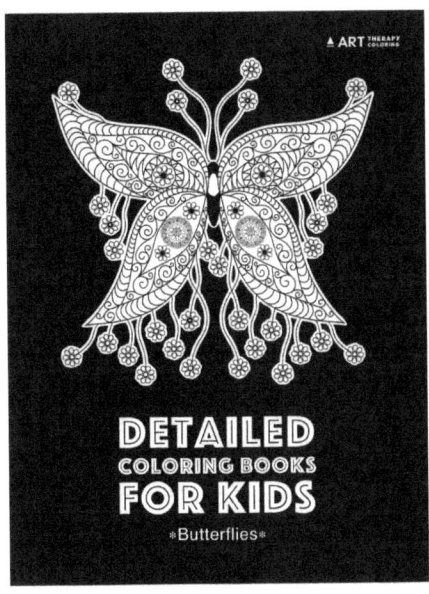

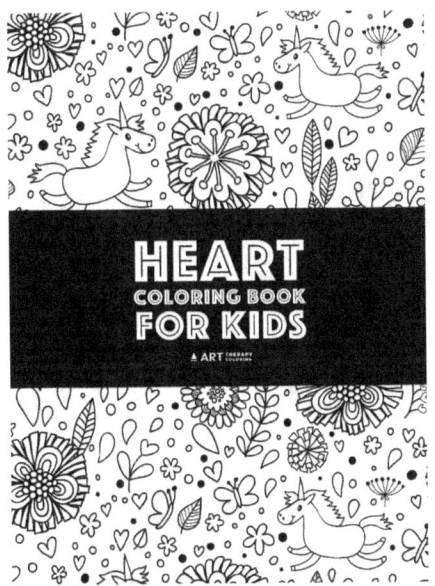

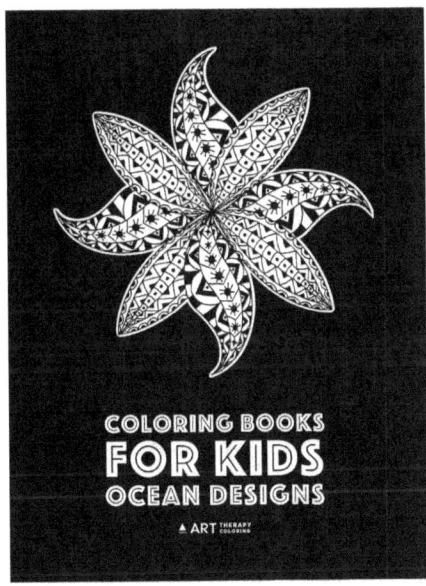

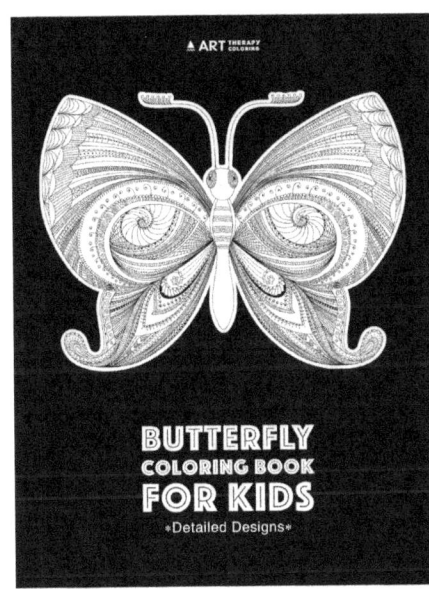

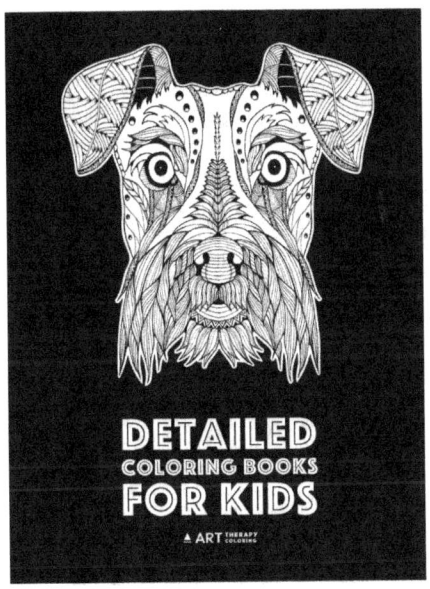

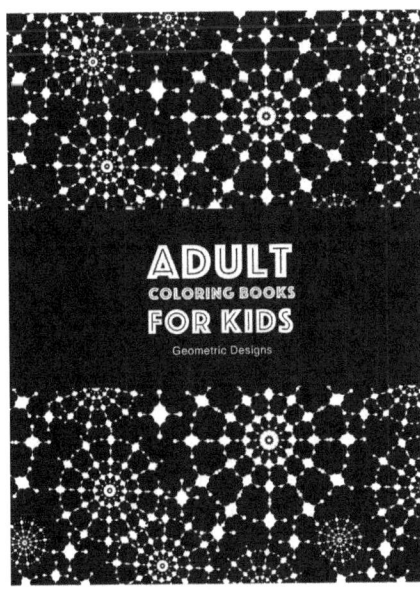

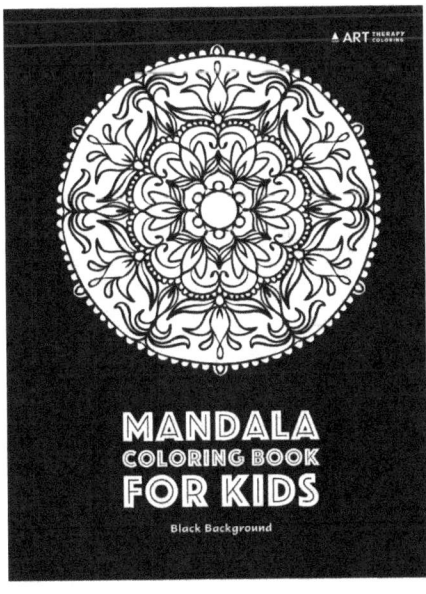

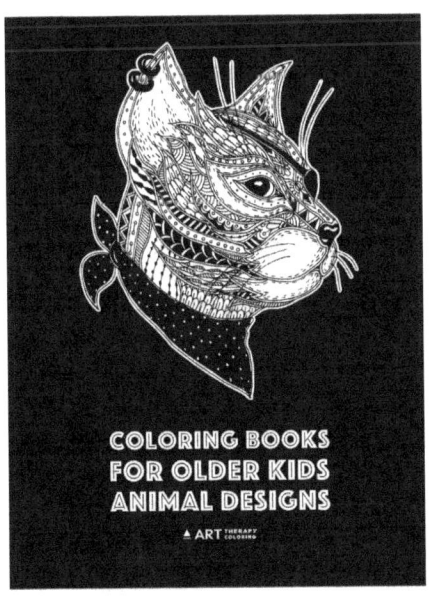

Coloring Books For Teens

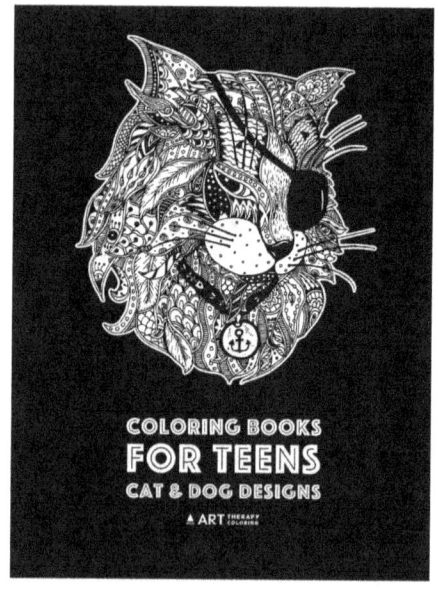

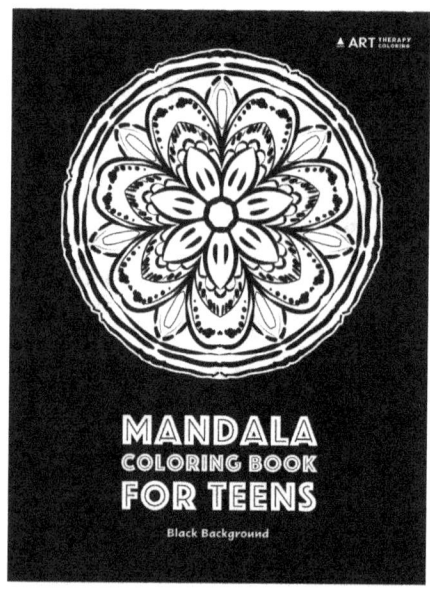

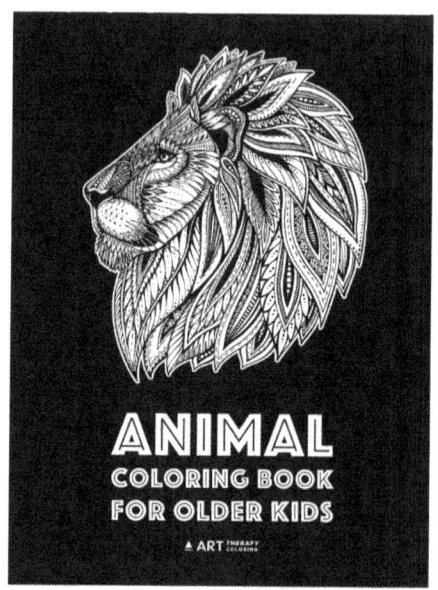

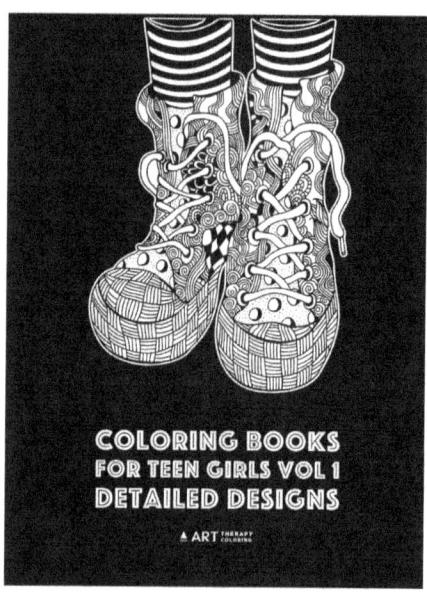

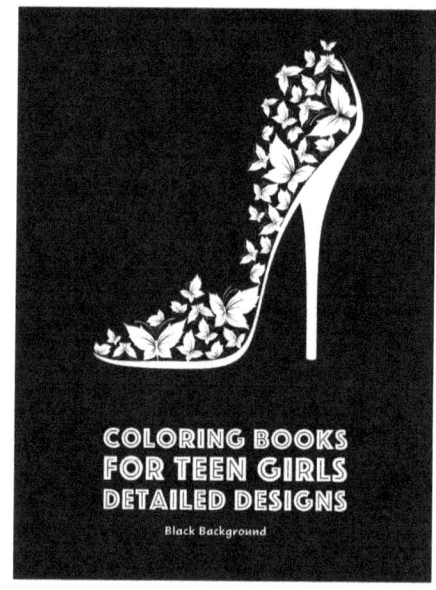

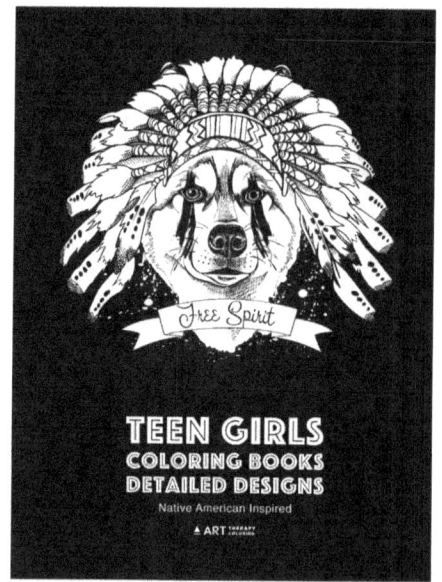

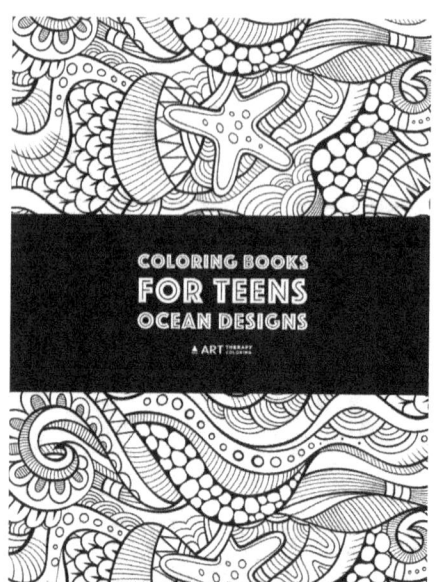

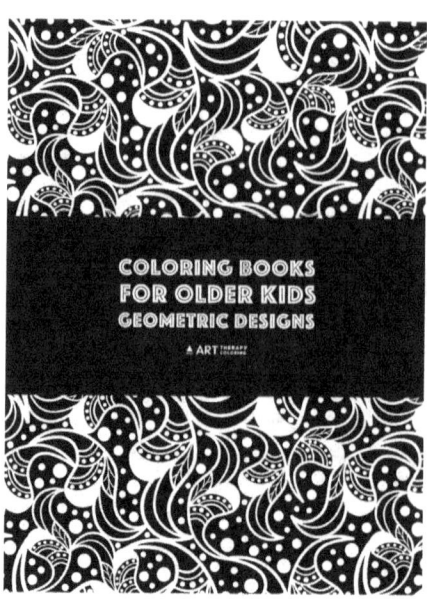

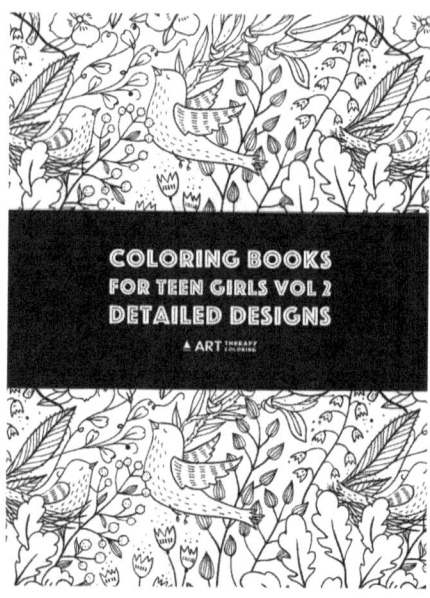

Coloring Books For Teens

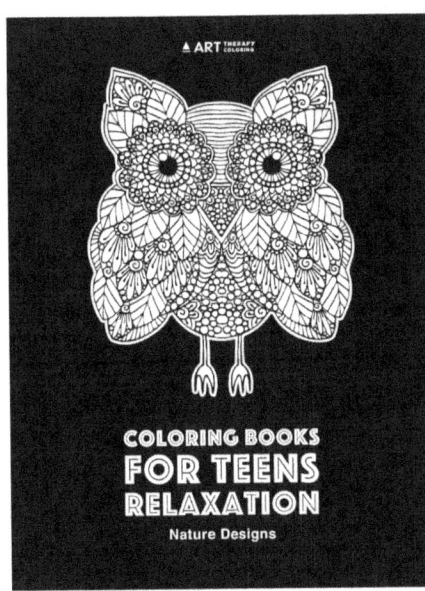

COLORING BOOKS FOR TEENS RELAXATION
Nature Designs

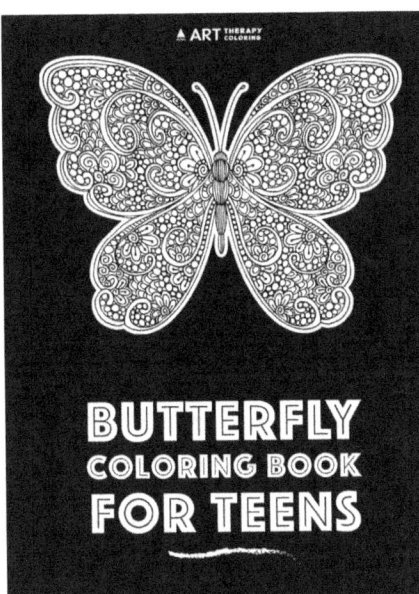

BUTTERFLY COLORING BOOK FOR TEENS

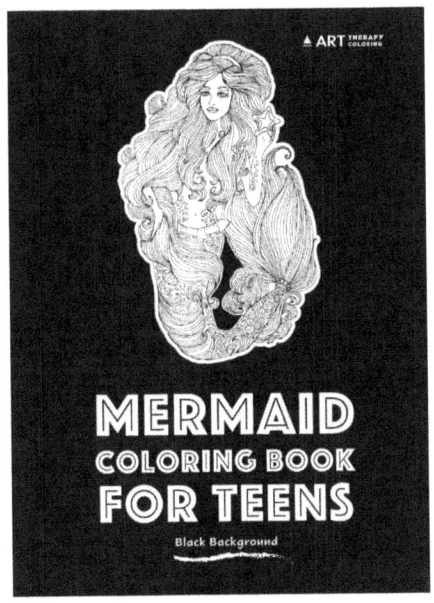

MERMAID COLORING BOOK FOR TEENS
Black Background

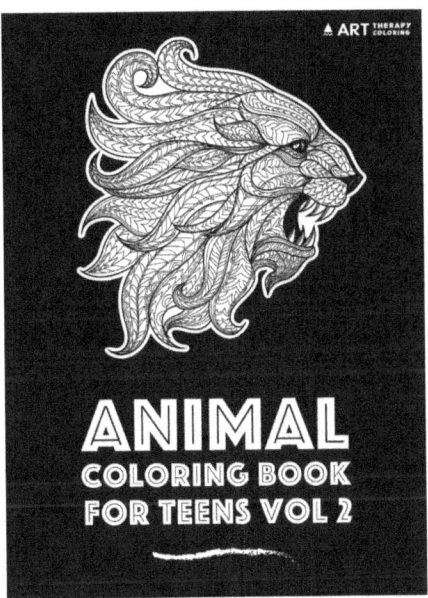

ANIMAL COLORING BOOK FOR TEENS VOL 2

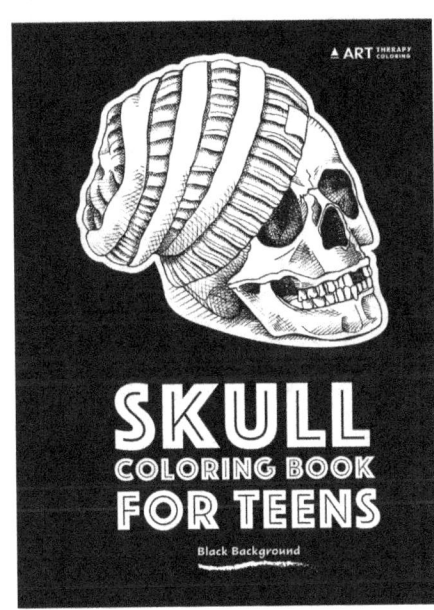

SKULL COLORING BOOK FOR TEENS
Black Background

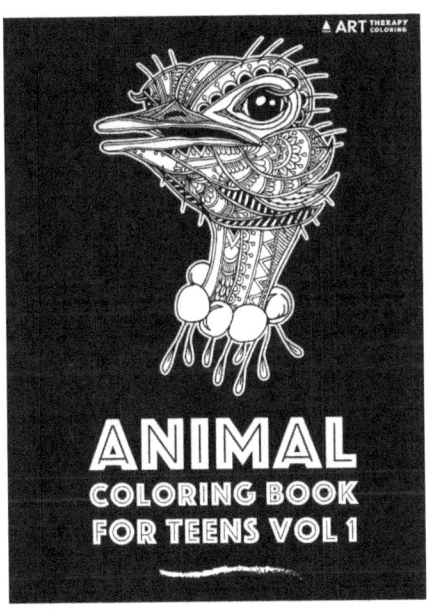

ANIMAL COLORING BOOK FOR TEENS VOL 1

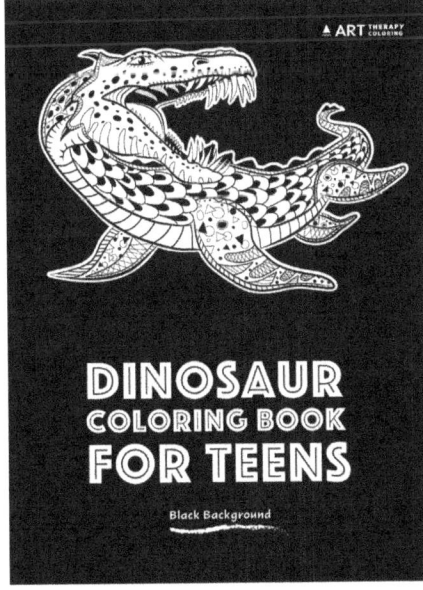

DINOSAUR COLORING BOOK FOR TEENS
Black Background

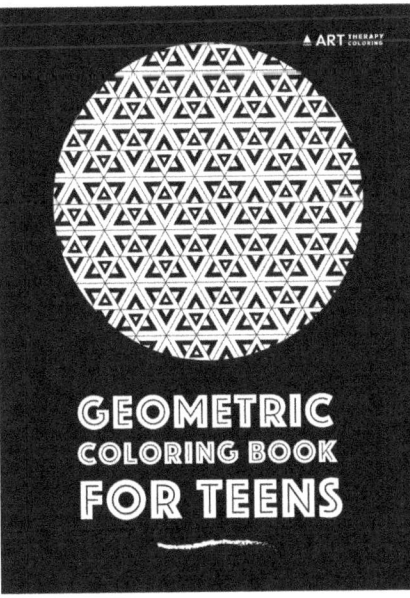

GEOMETRIC COLORING BOOK FOR TEENS

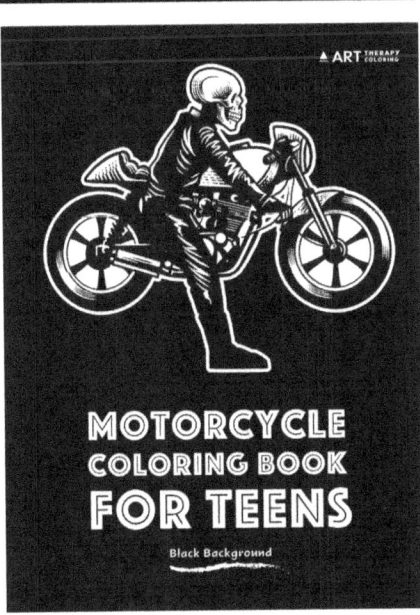

MOTORCYCLE COLORING BOOK FOR TEENS
Black Background

Coloring Books For Teens

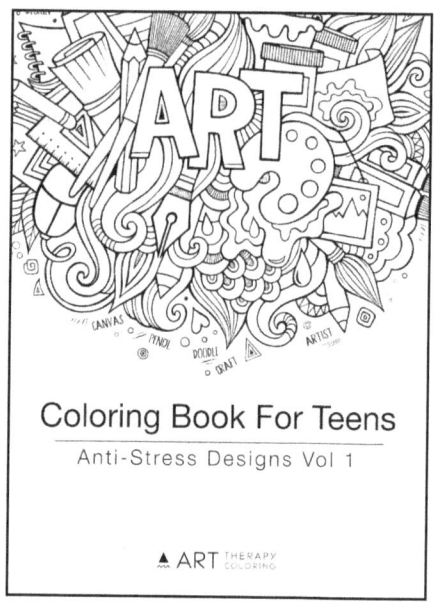

Coloring Book For Teens
Anti-Stress Designs Vol 1

▲ ART THERAPY COLORING

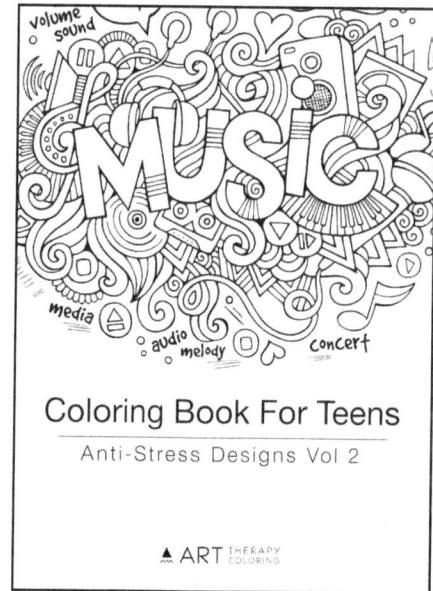

Coloring Book For Teens
Anti-Stress Designs Vol 2

▲ ART THERAPY COLORING

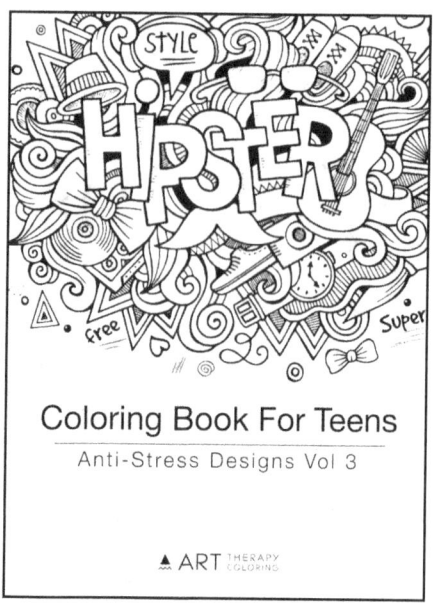

Coloring Book For Teens
Anti-Stress Designs Vol 3

▲ ART THERAPY COLORING

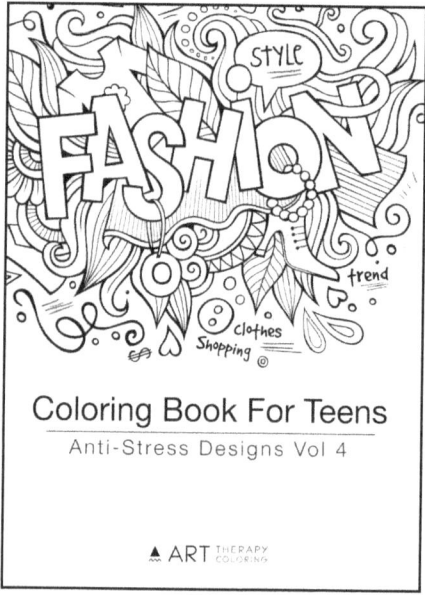

Coloring Book For Teens
Anti-Stress Designs Vol 4

▲ ART THERAPY COLORING

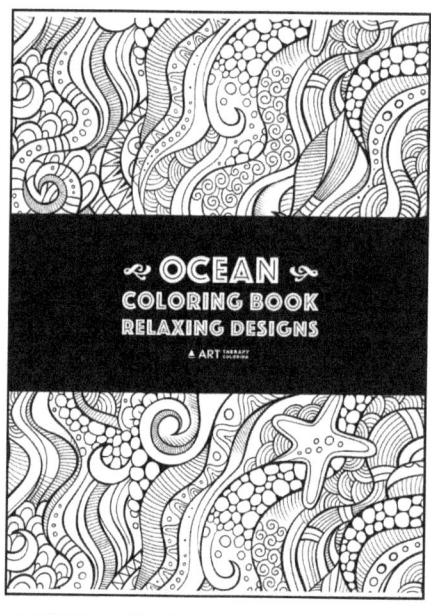

Coloring Book For Teens
Anti-Stress Designs Vol 5

▲ ART THERAPY COLORING

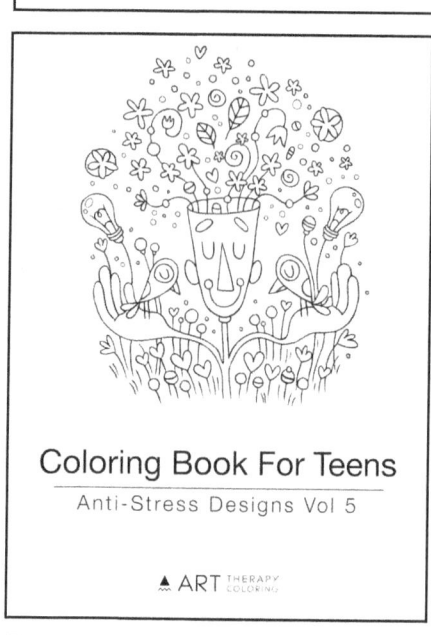

Coloring Book For Teens
Anti-Stress Designs Vol 6

▲ ART THERAPY COLORING

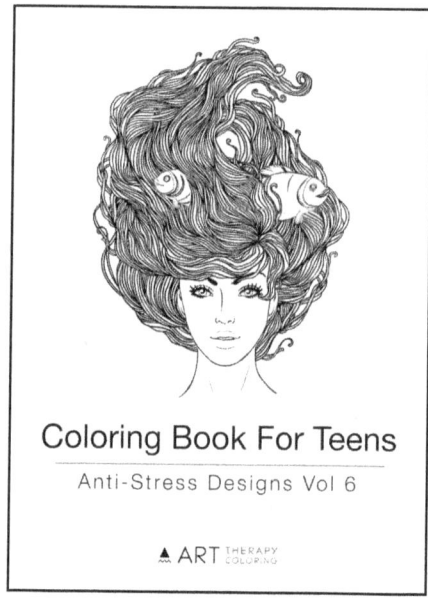

Coloring Book For Teens
Anti-Stress Designs Vol 7

▲ ART THERAPY COLORING

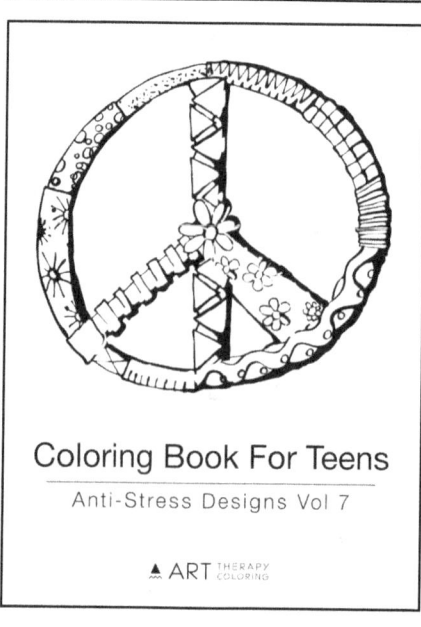

Coloring Book For Teens
Anti-Stress Designs Vol 8

▲ ART THERAPY COLORING

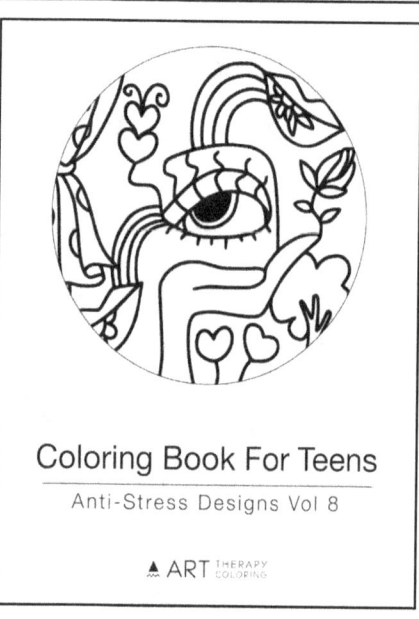

Coloring Books For Special Occasions

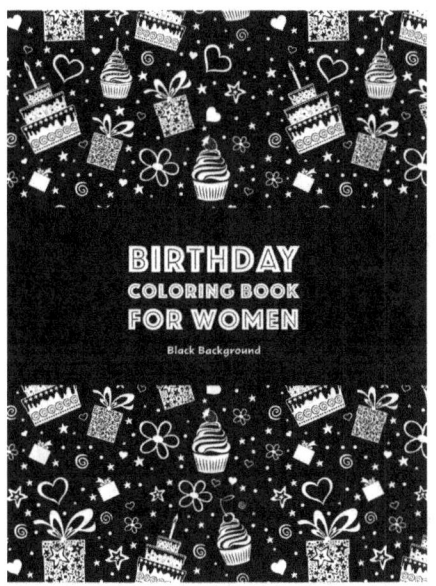

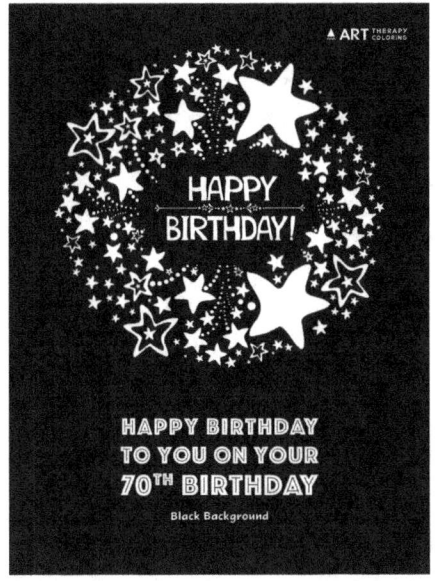

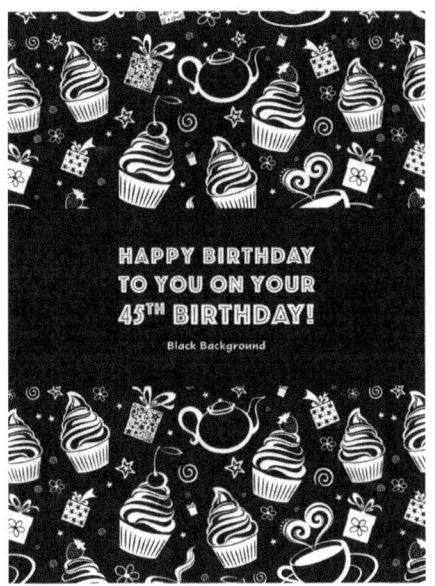

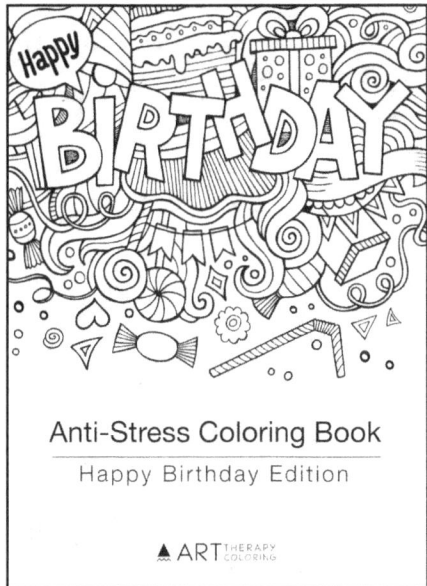

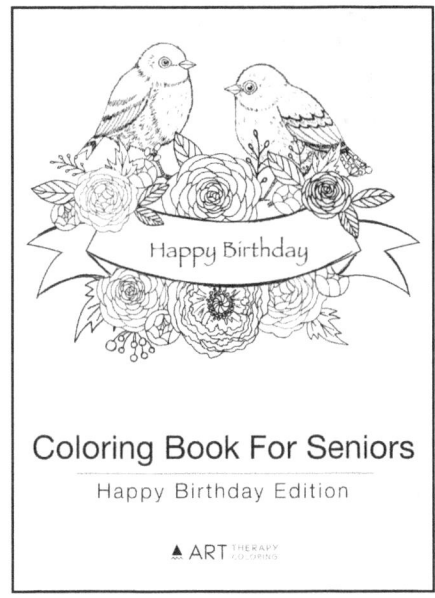

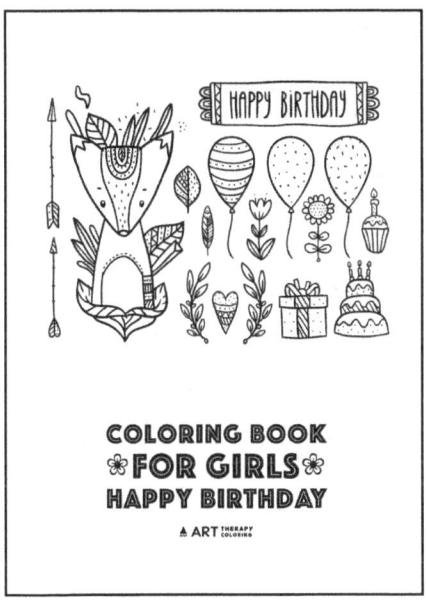

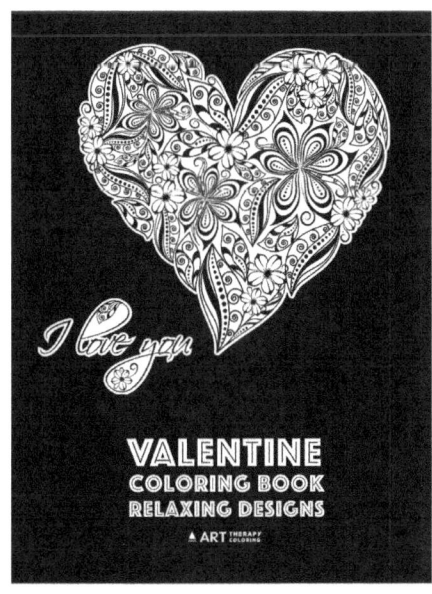

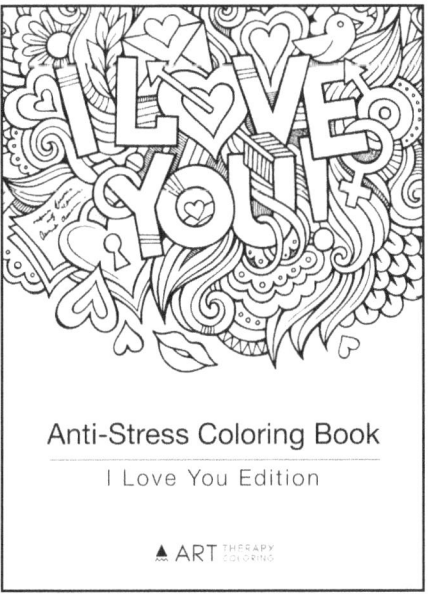

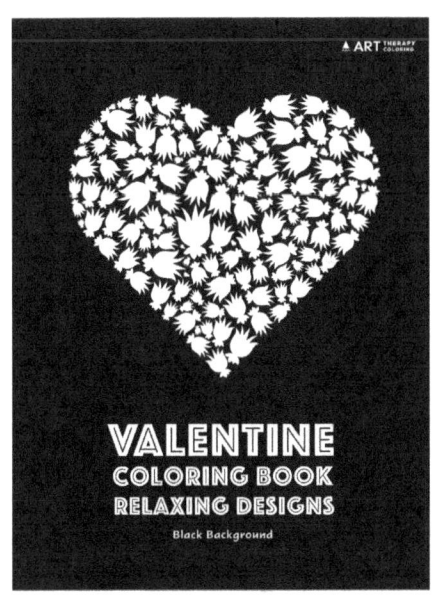

Coloring Books For Christmas

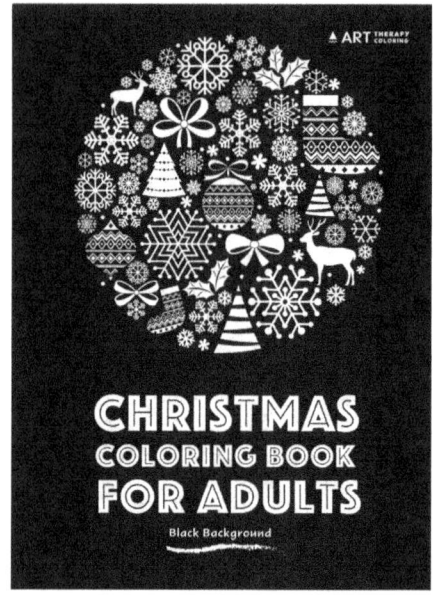

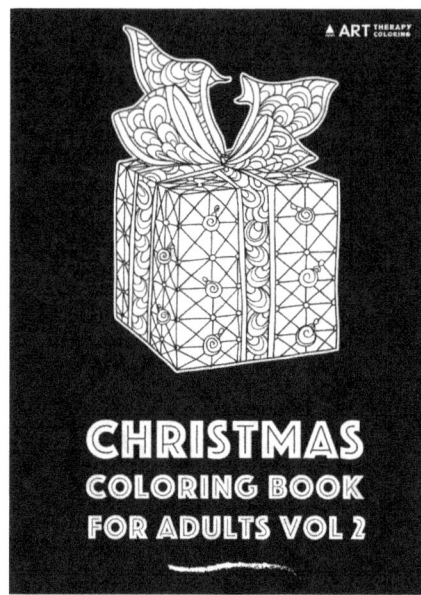

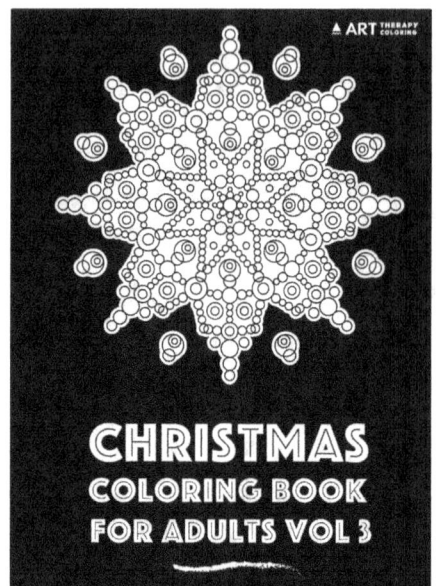

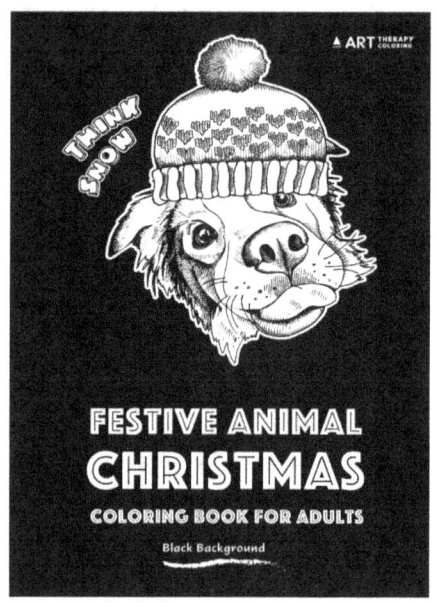

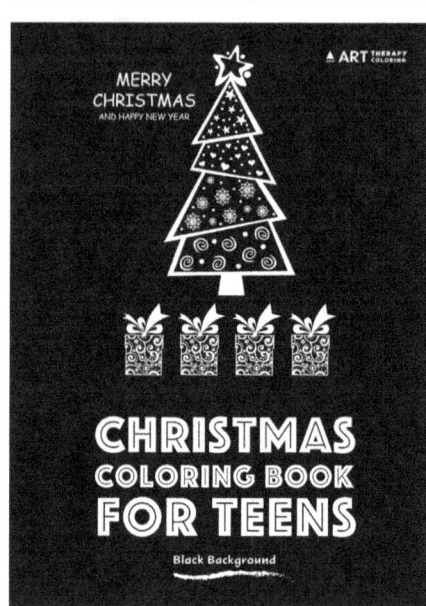

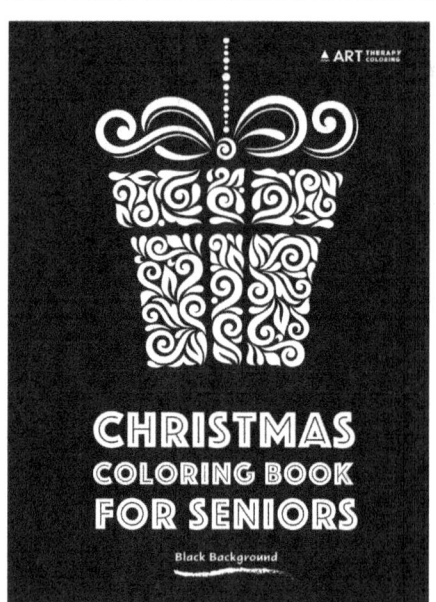

Skull Coloring Book For Adults

Published by:
Art Therapy Coloring
El Dorado Hills, California
www.arttherapycoloring.com

Shutterstock Images

ISBN: 978-1-64126-022-0

www.ingramcontent.com/pod-product-compliance
Lightning Source LLC
Chambersburg PA
CBHW081344180526
45171CB00006B/598